Forgotten Fife Tales

Jerzy T. Morkis

Forgotten Fife Tales
(A colourful cornucopia of reports, stories & forgotten tales
from the Kingdom of Fife)
First published 2020
Copyright © 2020 Jerzy T. Morkis
Email: fifetales@scotlandmail.com
Website: www.fifetales.com

ISBN: 978-0-244-85916-9

Cover photograph: Thomas Neil, coal miner, at home in Scoonie Drive, Leven, circa 1950. © Fife Tales.

A Colourful Cornucopia
of
Reports, stories
& forgotten tales
from the
Kingdom of Fife
Recounted from newspapers,
published journals
manuscripts and personal memories

Sourced, selected, collected, collated, edited and occasionally written by
Jerzy T. Morkis Esq, scrivener & journalist

A MORKIS & SPENCER PRODUCTION
PROUD PROMOTERS AND GALLANT DEFENDERS OF TYPOGRAPHY, PAPERS AND
INKS

DEDICATION

This collection of articles is dedicated to all the editors and reporters who produced publications that emerged from the communities they served: the men and women who knew getting the darts and dominoes results right was as important as that front page headline.

It is also dedicated to their real employers – the readers, ordinary folk who, day in and day out, were capable of being extraordinary. That was especially understood by the late Mike Delaney, a colleague and friend, who was as passionate about the title he served as I was about mine. He left us all too soon.

Everyone has a tale to tell, and a tale worth being told.

ACKNOWLEDGEMENTS

The articles in this collection were originally written for the launch of a proposed quarterly magazine that would have focused on Fife's history and heritage. Unfortunately that project was shelved but rather than these forgotten tales being buried again this publication allows them a brief moment in the sun.

It would not have been possible without the tolerance, patience and support of so many with whom I worked through the years. Special mention must go to Colin Hume, former editorial director with Johnston Press, who allowed me unlimited access to the bound volumes of the Fife weekly newspapers, and also shared in the joy of uncovering so many good stories from the past, and first gave an airing to 'They said they were Celtic' when he edited the Scottish Football Historian all those years ago.

The late Ian C. Paterson, as editor of the East Fife Mail, also instilled in me a near obsession with the local press, and ensuring that everything written was fair, accurate and balanced, as well as honest and precious.

I'm indebted to Melinda Gillen, editor of the Stornoway Gazette and its monthly publication Back in the Day, who trusted me to get it right when it came to exploring and sharing any historic tales that took my fancy from the Western Isles.

Finally, I'm indebted to my wife, Judith, who was happy to make Fife her home, and has tolerated, copy tasted and proofed all the stories of the Kingdom with which she has been regaled and bombarded.

CONTENTS

An introduction and a farewell to Uncle Jack

T he roots of this publication stretch back to the evening of Wednesday, April 29, 1936, and the columns of the Dundee Courier & Advertiser of Friday, May 1. It was on that midweek spring evening that my Uncle Jack was in a motorcycle accident. He never regained consciousness, dying the following morning, and, on the Friday, the Courier carried a short report on the fatal accident.

Every family has a tale to tell, and this one is no worthier or sorrowful than any other, and that's the point.

In this era of instant, global headlines, our local world of the past is being buried ever deeper.

My Uncle Jack is just one tiny part of that past. It is highly improbable anyone is aware of his brief story but its real significance is that neither was I, even though he was part of my family.

I was always aware of his name but the only physical memory I have of his entire life, and death, is a small, worn, barely legible grave marker in Leven's Scoonie cemetery that was pointed out to me when I was a child. I doubt I would be able to find it now.

John 'Jack' Neil was in his 20s and recently engaged to Jeanie when his life ended. He was actually my great-uncle but my mother, in her 90s, still remembered him with great affection.

She was just a child when he died. Raised by her grandparents, my mother remembers when the police knocked on the door and asked her to take them to the neighbour where her grandmother was visiting.

That was how the family learned Jack had been rushed to hospital after that road accident on the edge of Leven.

His death was a traumatic experience for his young niece and while she recalled the uncle who always had time to tease her and make her laugh, after 80 years the finer details of him had started to fade from her memory. And as to what happened on that fateful day, well, that seemed lost and a forgotten chapter in the Neil family history, until that newspaper report surfaced.

So much of all our history is lying buried and unread in the old columns of our local papers. You only need to look at the popularity of community Facebook pages to see how valued the people and places from our past are, not just for the warm glow of nostalgia but because they line the path we have taken to where we are now, and possibly provide an indication of what is ahead, certainly as far as the final truth is concerned.

Appreciating what and who are around you is really a big part of what we have, and who we are.

In the latter part of my career in local newspapers, when the titles were centralised, I was horrified to hear some young reporters after a telephone call dismissing a family member who had wanted an obituary in the local paper for a loved one.

"I mean he hadn't done anything," exclaimed one. "It wasn't like he was anyone ... important!"

Over the years I had tried to encourage more families to offer some details of those they had just lost. Everyone is important, and everyone has a story to tell, whether they have travelled and conquered the world, or never ventured beyond their village boundary.

Uncle Jack's short and ordinary life meant, by newsroom standards, he didn't merit an obituary in his local paper but thanks to the British Newspaper Archive and that edition of the Courier on Friday, May 1, 1936, I now know the details of his fateful last journey, and that, in itself, has sparked more memories for my mother and for all the family.

It was forgotten he worked down the pit ... and that he wanted out. He'd started a correspondence course and was making plans for a brighter future for himself and his bride-to-be. Was the motorbike and sidecar he was trying out part of his and Jeanie's independence?

And, having personally covered so many fatal accidents over the years, the little report in the Courier gives me an insight into that horrible day all those decades ago, and these few paragraphs moved my mother to tears as it brought the memories pouring back.

That was the power of local papers but it is a power that has been diminished and continues to diminish, because we have grudged the cover price to buy community relevance, forgotten that every story is important to someone.

We grudge paying for an online newspaper, and are happy to take news from sources where we have little or no connection, and where we have no real way to challenge its relevance, tone or interpretation.

The proprietors too must shoulder a share of the blame. While acknowledging newspapers are first and foremost a business and need to make money, the inability to come up with a viable commercial model that could marry local news with print and the new opportunities arising from the digital age is a sad indictment. Instead, the dwindling profit margins were defended by cuts, and that reduced readers and credibility, further reducing profit, and resulting in more cuts.

As with most of what we value, we won't really know how much we have lost until these local papers have faded away entirely.

On a personal level I discovered through them that my great-great-grandfather was lost at sea; I found the advertisement that my Polish father had to take out to announce his application to become a British citizen after the war; I read the report of my great-grandfather's accident down the pit ... and was able to confirm that my pal Douglas Seago and I came second in the three-legged race in Parkhill Primary's school sports.

Putting personal impact aside, it is forgotten that the local paper once prided itself as a journal of record.

It was a serious failing for a community event or issue to pass unnoticed, and rarely did a title struggle to fill its pages. Instead there was 'overmatter' where copy that could be held for a week would be saved.

There were also all sorts of typographical jiggery-pokery employed where fonts and point sizes were adjusted to squeeze in an extra few hundred words and ensure valued copy made that week's edition.

And, until the 1960s or later, pictures were a technical and time-consuming element, but the pages were still packed.

Even when photography became a key part of the news gathering process, the quest for blanket coverage continued. As one editor would tell his news team, "If it moves write about it; if it is standing still, photograph it."

As a result of that editorial diligence and determination, Fife's heritage is actually richer than most of us imagine. Those papers contain history the historians have missed, places that have disappeared from the map, personalities we have forgotten in our neighbourhoods ... and a million stories worth the retelling.

So, as a newspaper fan and 'dinosaur', I'm grateful to the reporter in 1936 who has allowed my mother more than 80 years later to say a final farewell to her favourite uncle and who introduced me to him properly.

I also forgive him and the sub-editor who handled the copy for muddling Uncle Jack's age.

LEVEN MAN FATALLY INJURED
Motor Cycle Burned Out After Collision

John Neil (27), Scoonie Drive, Leven, died in Wemyss Hospital yesterday morning as result of injuries sustained in a road accident the previous night. A motor cycle combination which he was driving was involved in a collision on the Lundin Links-Leven road with a car driven by John G. Marshall, journalist, Lochgelly.

Neil was having a trial run on the combination, which he intended to purchase from George Ross, Wellesley Road, Denbeath.

Ross was a passenger in the sidecar.

Neil was hurled against the windscreen and so severely injured that he never regained consciousness. After attention by Dr Wilson, Leven, he was rushed to hospital.

Ross sustained knee bruises and Marshall was unhurt.

The motor cycle combination, which was wrecked, caught fire and was burned out.

The front axle of the car was broken, and the right wheel, mudguard, door, and entire side of the vehicle were badly damaged.

Neil was 24 years of age, unmarried, and was employed at Wellesley Colliery, Denbeath. Recently he removed from Kennoway to reside with his brother in Leven.

A spot of colour
from our local correspondent

While local newspapers offer a rich insight into our community life of the past, they were also an intricate piece of information machinery. Today we think of eye-catching front pages, the dramatic 'splash', the sensational picture, the screaming headline, but those are comparatively new developments and rooted in the nationals as they fought to lure readers.

The true 'local' paper tended to be much more understated. It is also a fact that daily life, with all its horrors and hardships woven into the routine, was more readily accepted and consumed. A century or more ago, you'll find tucked away in columns stories that today would demand and command the front page, and would immediately be shared online and become the instant, and probably short-lived, buzz of social media.

But despite what grew into a credible source of information, the newspaper was always a commercial entity. Local news filtered its way into the national feeds that provided the readers with something extra between the adverts, and local advertising also provides a fascinating insight into the community life of its era.

Of course there were also the journalists, then very much part of those communities. They provided an understanding and awareness of local issues that have, in the main, now long passed. Esteemed editors like Malcolm Burness of the Fife Free Press, Ian Paterson of the East Fife Mail, and Duncan Campbell of the Fife Herald, lived shoulder to shoulder with their readers. Over the decades they provided their communities with a voice; not everyone would have agreed with the view expressed or the tone, but it had integrity, authority... and commanded trust.

But while the craft of the newsroom, the skills of the reporter and the commercial thrust of business provide a good snapshot of life below the dateline at the top of the page, there is one unsung hero whose input actually captures the true pulse of daily life – the correspondent.

At one time these district scribes were key members of staff. Some were paid a minor fee, many others wrote for free, with the newspaper's outlay simply being envelopes and a ream of copy paper. Over time, probably due to the diligence required, abuse encountered, financial cutbacks by newspaper management, editorial snobbery, as well as a failure to recognise their value, the correspondent gave way to the more convenient contributor. Usually this was the secretary of the woman's guild, the press officer of the Rotary Club etc. They served, and still serve, a purpose but that role is far removed from the correspondents who not only reported on the formal activities of their town or village, but had the freedom to wax lyrical on anything that took their fancy. Of course, the editor's pen could assign that deemed unsuitable to the spike but, generally, they were able to march to their own beat.

Fife had a solid tradition of such correspondents with the smaller communities in the east and north east of the Kingdom particularly suited for a resident scribe. It could be argued the Cupar-based Fife Herald was the last bastion of those proud, individualistic voices. The passing of Marianna Lines in 2018 saw the conclusion of a weekly commentary on Collessie life. Her distinctive submissions undoubtedly split the community but the demise of her reports also marked the end of an era for the Herald's district notes.

The district correspondent could, at times, be self-indulgent but his or her strength was being an accepted part of the community and, from that privileged bartizan, the extraordinary could be identified. As to whether you believe ordinary folk are capable of extraordinary deeds and episodes, or that each and every one of us are extraordinary in our own way, the district correspondent was able to give so many just a little of the recognition they merited, be that commendable deeds or simply horticultural prowess.

As a young reporter with the East Fife Mail I was fortunate to know many of those correspondents personally. I remember sitting in Alex (A.B.) Paterson's cosy study on a wintry Friday morning and watching the snow fall on Lade Braes as he rattled out his final piece of copy. This was the playwright whose 'Reunion in St Andrews' always drew my parents to the Byre Theatre when it was performed.

There was William 'Bill' Reid whose historical articles were a regular full-page feature in the Mail during the 1970s. We would have to nip along to his home in Lundin Links to pick up his copy, scrawled on foolscap lined paper, and take it back to the office where we would type it up. Given its academic weight and Bill's handwriting, it then had to be delivered, along with his original, for him to check. These wordy features not only improved our knowledge of local history but developed our Latin.

For some reason I seemed to inherit this duty more than most and, as a result, got to know the former headmaster quite well. He was impressed when he learned I had taken religious studies as part of my degree and was happy to blether away about Hinduism and Buddhism between tutoring me on such subjects as the economic importance of Methil Docks in the 19th century.

In one exchange on the Vedas, he asked where and when I had learned to read Sanskrit. I explained that all my studies had involved English translations; he seemed disappointed and disapproving. On seeing me to the door when I was leaving, he advised me I really should take the trouble to learn Sanskrit as I would get so much more out of those great works if I interpreted them for myself. Bill also thought a more intense study of Latin and Greek was important for an inquisitive reporter. Yet, despite his academic prowess, and, with the greatest respect, a degree of self-indulgence, he was also a firm believer in his local newspaper. Among his last words, shortly before he died, was, "Tell the Mail there won't be an article next week."

You couldn't get further removed from Bill's table in Lundin Links, piled high with tomes of historical works, to the kitchen table of Mrs Coventry in East Wemyss.

She was a traditional district correspondent. Folk would drop into her miner's cottage in Approach Row and she would transcribe their little reports on to copy paper. She knew what was coming from each of her contacts, and when, so it wasn't unusual to be given a seat at her hearth and a cup of tea while she waited for a straggler from some local group or organisation to arrive with a weekly update.

It would be hard to overestimate the esteem these contributors and correspondents were held in by the newspaper, by advertising and editorial. They were essentially our representatives in their communities, and that produced a close and trusted bond. Up until the 'digital' revolution, which allowed newsrooms to write straight to the page, the papers even employed people who were tasked, as a large part of their remit, to handle these contributions. These sub-editors practised a dark art of symbols and numbers, like hieroglyphics, that magically produced bold print, italics, point size and typefaces but the very heart of their job was to correct any mistakes. Of course this was important for the paper but even more so for the correspondent. Their columns each week gave them credibility in their own communities, and they trusted the paper to spot the spelling or grammatical mistakes, as well as any howlers, ensuring their own distinct voice maintained its authority.

Depending on the handwriting that process would see copy passing from club secretary to correspondent to reporter to sub-editor to compositor to proof reader, and then possibly even being checked again on the page by the editor or chief reporter.

On the rare occasions that anything untoward slipped through, it would be the paper that took the blame, the justification wasn't that it should have been spotted but to ensure the correspondent remained blameless, and maintained the trust of those who fed into him or her.

While there might be occasions when there was gnashing of teeth as a submitted piece of copy was passed from one reporter to another in a bid to decipher some illegible word, you never, ever mocked the spelling, a typographical error or an unintended double entendre. If someone had taken the time and trouble to compile a report for, say, a Salvation Army meeting, held on a Saturday night for the town's elderly and lonely, and you were caught ridiculing the prose, then you could expect a dressing down from the editor and compulsory attendance with your notebook at those meetings for the rest of the session. Scunner any group and you risked losing all its members as readers and potential advertisers, losing your correspondent and tarnishing the paper's reputation as the voice of the community.

The fishing village of St Monans had a long and impressive record of correspondents who served the local press. In the 1970s and '80s, the sisters Jean and Margaret Robertson recorded virtually anything that moved in the burgh, even joining community groups specifically to generate reports. On their retirement they were succeeded by the former provost, Councillor James Braid. As a man of strong opinion, his hand-written pages of reports, collected every Monday for the East Fife Mail, offered a unique, and sometimes personal, view of events in St Monans, and, as a local, his knowledge provided a context stretching back through the decades.

Impressive though these correspondents were, their predecessors were just as remarkable, and anonymous. It would seem John Jack, author of 'An historical account of St Monance ...' (1844), regularly populated the columns of the Fife Herald. Though the contributions are unattributed, the timescale, the use of language, and the unique view of community life would all indicate Jack was a significant contributor.

8

While the author seemed equally at ease using his 'St Monance' (as it was then) label to comment on national events or criticising the authorities' efforts in dealing with crimes, suspected or real, the day-to-day life of the village was also chronicled.

And one area where correspondents reigned supreme was the obituary. Their knowledge of folk they met on a daily basis was of a depth unimaginable to a reporter just a few miles along the road.

And if anyone doubts everyone has a life worth noting, here is (most likely) Jack's obituary to Charles Pink which appeared in the Fife Herald in August 1849.

Sudden Death: *On Wednesday last week, one of our fellow-citizens, named Charles Pink, was suddenly summoned to quit all connexion with this fluctuating scene of existence.*

Being a member of that reeling, roaring, ranting fraternity called cadgers, he was traversing the country on Tuesday in the procession of a herring vending expedition and, on Wednesday, he was stretched out in the stillness of death, and arrayed in the habiliments of the grave.

Charles, in his youth, belonged to that peculiar society, commonly clad in scarlet livery, who are trained and disciplined in the science of legal murder, and who deliberately sally forth at the behest of crowned heads for the express purpose of slaying men whom they never saw, and avenging quarrels, of which they are perfectly ignorant.

The demise of our fellow-townsman has effected no saving to the country, as his name was not honoured with a place in the pension list; and, after spending the vigour of his life in the service of his king, was dismissed to provide for himself and family in the best way he could.

His first adventure in the cadging line was attended with total failure. He wended his way to Cupar with an ass laden with partans which he considered a bright speculation; but having set up the cry of partans within the precinct of the county town and aroused the lovers of shellfish, Charles had none to produce – the crawlers having contrived to effect their escape by the way.

Charles was a peaceable subject, though an admirer of the spirit-stirring productions of Sir John Barleycorn, and his periodical libations in honour of the jolly knight generally lasted for a fortnight; but under which he uniformly evinced a disposition to preach rather than quarrel or wrangle with his neighbours.

That truly is a memorable literary send-off, but the obituary can also offer up tales stranger than fiction, again of seemingly ordinary people who had experienced the extraordinary.

Though after Jack's time, this obituary from the Fife Herald in 1870 again came from the pen of a St Monans correspondent.

Headed 'The Romance of Life', it details the life of a well-kent resident, George Mathers, who had died at the age of 86. That was a grand age for an East Neuk fisherman but this passing of a respected 'salty dog' saw details emerge of another remarkable chapter in his story that overshadowed the hard life endured at the nets.

George's father, who was a miner in the coal pits, died young, leaving a widow and three children wholly to the care of Providence.

But with that blessing on her own brave self-reliant heart, the poor mother struggled through until the boys were able to earn a crust for themselves.

George, the oldest, took to a sea life, and like everybody else in those days of blank draves and dull shipping, went to Greenland as a whaler. He was so employed in one of the Dunbar ships, when, on the return voyage, he, along with nearly twenty others belonging to St Monance or the neighbourhood, were " pressed" by the war brig Cruizer, from which was soon after drafted a squadron then being fitted for attack on the French coast.

George Mathers was in the boats when a night attack was made on one of the enemy's seaports but, a violent gale having sprung up, the British flotilla was cast ashore, and the unfortunate party were taken prisoners of war.

This was in 1803, when our hero was only nineteen years of age; but though a mere lad, so great was the terror of the French at the British by sea, that he and the rest of the shipwrecked sailors were compelled to walk forty miles before they were allowed to rest or sleep, when they were taken to Valcennes {Valenciennes}, when he passed ten years and six months in the wearisome French prison.

Often, we may be assured, in the dull and cheerless prison, would the poor captive yearn to be once more with the beautiful green shores of Fife, and often would the tears come at the thought of his mother and friends in the old home; but the cruel war gave no hope of deliverance, and, day by day, his young spirit fretted and chaffed like the caged bird, but, like it, all in vain for liberty.

The prisoners were huddled together, and though they went occasionally and played at football or other pastime, yet, a natural consequence of so many men of different tastes and temper, being all brought into one place, they fought and quarrelled almost every hour.

Though dark as the picture was, it was not wholly without a gleam of light. There was a navigation school within the walls, taught by an English officer, which George Mathers was in the habit of attending, though he often spoke of himself as one the idlest and wildest of all the English prisoners.

A beautiful anecdote, however, can be told of him at this time. Though the French fleets were swept from the sea, their privateers often succeeded by stratagem in capturing a stray merchant ship even at the mouth of the harbour. One of these captures was a brig bound from London to Hull, on board of which was a youth, fourteen, going to visit his friends in the latter place, but who, with the crew of the vessel, was sent as prisoner to Valcennes.

The first sight of the poor, trembling, English boy, so like his own little brother at home, touched the heart of our hero, who, from that hour, adopted him as a son – watching over him at all times with more than fatherly tenderness and care.

Though comparatively careless himself about education, he took especial interest in the instruction of the lad, whose singular progress was no less the delight of the accomplished master who presided over the school. This boy, grown into a handsome young man, returned to England on being released at the Peace, and so liberal had his education been that he became the tutor, and subsequently the head master, of a high-class seminary near London.

He became the father of a family of divines and teachers, and on one occasion sent for his benefactor, George Mathers, when a fisherman in St Monance, whom he placed at the head of his table before his children to whom he told the story, concluding – "It is not to me but to this noble man you are indebted for everything."

After remaining over ten years in prison, George at length succeeded in making his escape, and was doing his best to reach the coast, hiding by day and travelling by night – when the abdication of Napoleon in 1814 brought the return of peace, when he came back to St Monance, where, with the exception of a short service in the revenue cutters and an occasional voyage, he passed his long day as a fisherman – most respected and most esteemed by those who knew him best.

11

Though a man of reserved manners and little speech, yet, like his gifted brother Thomas, the poet fisherman, he had deep and earnest sympathies, and a wonderful familiarity with Allan Ramsay, and the other great poets of Scotland.

The tales of Pink and Mathers could hardly be more diverse, but that's the magic of the local newspaper columns. While those penned tributes forever capture their presence and passing but only hint at their full story, the thrill is that there are others waiting to be discovered; the sadness is that so many more departed, and continue to depart, without acknowledgement or recognition of their contributions, be it to kin, community or country.

Of course, village correspondents were primarily concerned with the living and events as they unfolded in front of them. That primary role saw them very much as "our man on the spot" and, in that position, the village news columns across the country are littered with fascinating insights and bizarre observations. As to why this Fife Herald correspondent in 1850 chose to recount this anecdote from a few years previous is unknown but it is a fitting example of the unique role the village contributor as observer once had.

During the lucumbency of Dr Chalmers at Kilmany, he sometimes officiated at Kennoway. On one of these occasions among his hearers was Jean Pirie, a tall, masculine-looking woman, generally dressed in a red cloak with a black hood, with a staff in her hand, who went about as a vagrant, and was considered the Madge Wildfire of the district. Jean dearly loved a dram; and when she had the means often indulged to excess. She had got a 'drop' before going to church when Dr Chalmers delivered a brilliant discourse from the words 'Look not on the wine when it is red', and, some of his words displeasing Jean, she rose up in the middle of the sermon, pointed her cudgel at the Doctor, and exclaimed: 'Stop! Stop! Gies nane o' your German language here!' The Doctor stopped, the audience was amazed, and the Rev Mr Wright, the minister of the parish, rose and remarked that was an example of the vice against which the Doctor was animadverting, and forthwith ordered George Anderson, the beadle, to put Jean out of the church. Jean resisted, spoke, struggled, and flourished her staff but, at length, George, with the assistance of some of the congregation, got her put to the door, when the Doctor resumed his eloquent sermon.

The editor who waited 50 years to share a secret

Given the headlines it has received in recent years, what became known as 'Buckhaven's Secret Tragedy' could not fall into the category of a forgotten Fife tale, though, like much local history, younger readers may be oblivious to a story that is still within living memory for a few.

The term 'secret' was applied to this horrific naval mine explosion because there was no public acknowledgement or record of it for 50 years. We will never know if it would ever have come to light had it not been for the East Fife Mail. While it is true to say every national, and international, headline, is a local story somewhere, it is unusual for a local 'exclusive' to be 50 years old.

The Mail's publication of the tale was in the days before web searches and social media so even establishing it was indeed a 'secret' was a challenge in itself.

While the details of the tragedy now sit in the archives of the local, regional and national press, and there is even a modest memorial at Buckhaven's Bank Corner, unveiled in 2006, there is a background to the story's emergence into the public domain, and that could easily be forgotten. Only a few people know the circumstances surrounding uncovering the tragedy and, given the horror of the central events, these have little importance, but still deserve a place just for the record.

As editor of the Mail in 1991 and author of that original story, together with the chief reporter Colin Hume, later to become the award-winning editor of the Falkirk Herald, we are probably best placed to provide that background.

The real credit for the story finally being made public goes to the Mail's editor 50 years before – the late William (Bill) Phenix. Thanks to Andrew J. Campbell, of Fife Family History Society, I later learned Phenix was the nominal editor of the 'Leven Liar' from 1939-1949. However, he also served in the Intelligence Corps during World War Two and during the period that he was away the Leven Mail, as it was then, was edited by his father, William snr.

So, as local newspapermen, father and son would have been only too aware of the Buckhaven incident, and the regulations governing press freedom during these dark years. Curtailing outrage and maintaining morale would have been a priority so reporting restrictions smothered the circulation of the story. It would have been limited to word of mouth, delivered in whispers, and, as Britain desperately fought for survival, there were tragic tales a-plenty to keep the public occupied.

That containment seems to have worked but those who witnessed the event, and its immediate aftermath, would not, and could not, forget, so the story remained alive, albeit within an ever-decreasing circle.

Of course, someone who would have known and talked to many on the scene in 1941 was Phenix, both or either of them. In 1991, 50 years after the tragedy, Bill resolved that something should be done so the community could learn the names of the children who perished, and ensure they were remembered.

Most local newspaper offices have now disappeared through the centralisation of production and they never held a monument to their past staff. There were no boards listing the lineage of editors, no roll of honour of reporters or advertising managers. Given the very nature of small newspapers, deadline day remains unaffected by an employee's departure, or even death. Everyone is expendable; it is the title that must always be tended, not its temporary servants.

So when a brief letter, signed by William Phenix but with no contact details, dropped through the letterbox of the East Fife Mail's office at 7 Mitchell Street, Leven, with the barest outline of the tragedy, I had no idea who he was, or the credibility of the events he outlined. Given he was from a family of journalists one would have thought some embellishment would have come naturally, and added to the reliability of the claims. Why he chose to keep his revelation so brief, though detailing the names of the victims, remains a mystery.

And, historically, there was a further complication. Just five months before the Buckhaven explosion, in January 1941, a similar tragedy had occurred four miles along the road on the shoreline of West Wemyss. There a sea mine was spotted and five locals, including a teenager, tried to push it away from the village but it detonated, killing them all. The two tales inevitably became entwined.

Of the few tools of trade a reporter has, the most important by far is, or at least was, his or her contact book containing the names, addresses and telephone numbers of the sources that helped fill the paper every week. The arrival of a phone on every desk, replacing the communal call box, saw reporters regularly ringing around their connections to ask: "Just wondering if anything's been happening?"

The Mail's news team's efforts to confirm, never mind expand, the details of the Phenix letter produced little result from those contacts. Local politicians and official sources could shed no light on the tale and, of course, the paper's bound volume from the year gave nothing away.

But a breakthrough came from Methil Writers' Workshop when one of the organisers revealed that the Buckhaven tragedy was the subject selected by one of its members, Myra Frantz. She was just seven when it occurred but the memories of that day had not faded.

Colin Hume and I spent the weekend trying to piece together the story. Records from the Co-operative's funeral services confirmed the deaths and burials, but most of the contacts we spoke to were incredulous that such a tragedy had occurred on their doorsteps and they had never heard of it. But there were those who had heard snippets and rumours. So the jigsaw started to come together, and the horror of that day stepped for the first time into the light for all of Levenmouth.

That produced a strong reaction and generated a few more details, some too graphic and disturbing to publish. 'Buckhaven's Secret Tragedy' finally took its place in Fife history and has continued to evolve through its recounting in Scottish regional dailies and a widening website presence. Even the Sunday Times in 2005 carried a feature on this incident in Britain's 'secret war'. By the time the Levenmouth Regeneration Initiative unveiled a memorial plaque on Remembrance Sunday in 2006, parts of the story were being rewritten.

Fife Today, the website of the Fife group of newspapers of which the East Fife Mail is a part, in a report in 2015, drawing on new research, discounted aspects of Myra Frantz's recollections and gave a new Christian name to one of the victims.

Though, understandably, interest in the story has waned, it is possible the events of the day will evolve further as more memories emerge, though time is not on the side of these to be living testimonies.

However, trusting today's and tomorrow's journalists to continue to adjust the record of events, I will adhere primarily to the version the Mail carried in 1991, built around those who were there and shared their trauma. It published on Wednesday, June 5, 1991.

The previous Sunday (June 2) had marked the 50th anniversary of the tragedy that had claimed 10 lives, eight of them children.

In 1941, June 2 fell on a Monday and, despite the tension of the war years, the day offered a chance to relax and enjoy the festivities of the Fife Miners' Gala, with the annual parade a major and eagerly anticipated attraction.

That morning, many of the youngsters were already out and about, a number of them down on the shore by the locally-dubbed 'Jawbanes', playing and skiffing stones.

One man, who insisted on speaking to the Mail anonymously, was scouring the water's edge for any sea coal that he could take home for the fire.

"I noticed what I thought, at first, was the back of a dead dog," he said. "As the tide was on the ebb I had a sack half full of coal. There was something I took to be a mooring buoy so I dumped my sack of coal on top of that.

"Then two boys appeared. I managed to fill my sack; then I was able to see what the thing was. It was about four feet long and as broad as a man's back."

The area was surrounded with deep mud and, not being aware of how dangerous the object was, the man headed home to get ready for work.

It would seem these two lads were soon joined by another six of their pals, and they decided to haul the object clear. It's possible the boys, motivated by the government's salvage drive to collect metal, believed their find could help the war effort. But whatever their reason, they decided to drag it ashore.

Myra Frantz picked up the story there: "My Uncle Bobby {Birrell} had a stable, horses and a sea coal business.

"He was having his usual blether with the scaffy when he saw the boys. He shouted to them to 'get rid of that thing' as it didn't look safe."

What happened next remains uncertain. Some heard the lads tried to lift the object upright, others that it was about to be loaded onto a cart, or, as in the Frantz version, it was being heaved across the cobbled stable yard.

"It exploded," she wrote, "causing havoc and mayhem. The old houses withstood the blast from the mine but their walls were embedded with pieces of shrapnel.

"There had been ten boys and men at the stables that morning. Eight died immediately. The huge wooden doors were blown off and, inside, two horses died where they stood.

"There was a huge crater in the yard, boulders everywhere. It was a scene of complete disaster. The scaffy, who was inside the stable at the time of the blast filling up his water can to make tea, was the only one to survive."

The two other adults on the scene would die from their injuries, Henry Wilkie (37) the next day, and Bobby Birrell on June 4, giving him time to share his version of events with his family, thus providing the source of his niece's recollections.

The remains of most of those who died in the horrific explosion were laid to rest in the parish cemetery at East Wemyss where simple headstones gave no clue as to the circumstances of their death. The only acknowledgement permitted appeared in a regional daily newspaper at the end of the week which simply stated that the provost had launched a disaster fund.

It seems any subsequent inquiry into events went unreported in the local community. The families who suffered a loss were left to be comforted by their neighbours and Buckhaven was forced to hold on to its 'secret'. Those who died, with the names later being inscribed on Buckhaven war memorial, were Robert Birrell (31), George Irvine (13), George Jensen (15), Robert Jensen (14), Joe Kinnear (13), William Kinnear (10), John Thomson (12), Henry Walton (14), Henry Wilkie (37), James Wilkie (13).

The Frantz version concluded: "On the day of the mass funeral, a company of Polish soldiers stationed in Leven were out on a march which happened to coincide with the departure of the hearses. They stood to attention and gave a salute.

"The streets of Buckhaven were lined with people that day and the crowds seemed to stretch all the way to East Wemyss and to the cemetery. Many were school chums of the boys who died: it was a sight never to be forgotten."

There is a sad footnote to this tragic story, and that concerns Bill Phenix, the editor who waited 50 years for his title to recognise those who had been lost.

In April 1999, Bill (88) and his sister Mary Hutchison (82) were out for a drive and stopped at the nature reserve at Birnie Loch, near Collessie. At around 4pm, their car shot forward and then plunged down an embankment and into the loch. Efforts to reach them proved futile and both drowned in their vehicle.

Bustle and bother on the buses and a one-armed hero

When it comes to nostalgia, in the battle between bus and train the latter always wins by a mile. That's a bit ironic because when the Beeching cuts struck in the 1960s there wasn't really a public outcry at the tracks being lifted. More and more folk were picking up their first set of car keys and an intricate network of bus routes saw a 'halt' sign in just about every street that made commuting easy and inexpensive.

But there are certain similarities to the trains today and the buses of yesteryear. No-one likes the discomfort of standing room only on a train, which is probably the last form of public transport where being crammed in like sardines is a fairly regular occurrence.

Of course, if it happens to be the last train then the tolerance level does increase considerably; after all, uncomfortable though it may be, it beats being abandoned on a platform or having to fork out on a taxi fare.

Before health and safety regulations, the bus was also one mode of transport with serious passenger congestion, especially if it was the last one and coincided with chucking out time ... and clocking in time at the pit.

In 1926 the issue of overloading, particularly on the Leven to Kirkcaldy route, was becoming a major concern, so much so that the courts' view was that the long arm of the law should be summoned to reach out and hoik the excess passengers off.

That was easier said than done, at least according to one court case in early April 1926.

The incident, as reported in the Fife Free Press & Kirkcaldy Guardian, saw bus driver James Rintoul Smith, St Clair Street, and conductress Helen Donaldson, Nether Street, both Kirkcaldy, up before Sheriff Dudley at Cupar, charged with breaking the law on Sunday, February 28, by allowing 46 passengers on board when the bus was built to hold just 20.

Represented by R.N. Robertson of Cupar, both entered pleas of not guilty with their mitigation being they were simply providing a public service and no-one was going to take any heed of being told to lighten the load in any case.

One can imagine the cramped conditions on board the bus must have been bordering on the intimate when Police Sergeant Park tried to squeeze aboard in Aberhill. The officer had flagged it down after the driver spotted him, switched off the inside lights and failed to stop at the Tower Bar.

Sgt Park managed to get 11 passengers to disembark before he could clamber inside and count the remaining 35.

The prosecution dismissed the claims that the conductress, and driver, hadn't been able to do anything to halt the flood of fares as it was believed they could have easily got off and summoned the police. One can only assume Ms Donaldson managed to retain a space near the door.

One passenger, who had been heading home to East Wemyss, confessed to the court that he knew the bus was full but decided it was better to hang on than walk home, and he admitted he wouldn't have paid any heed to the conductress telling him to get off anyway.

Described by the court reporter as a "rosy-cheeked lass of small stature", Ms Donaldson told the court everything was in order with all seated when there was a sudden rush that she was powerless to stop. Among them were a good number of miners who had to clock on for the 10pm nightshift.

"What am I against a lot of men on the last bus?" she asked the sheriff.

Mr Smith, the driver, said that after Sgt Park took all the passengers' names, he "put them back again".

"Do you expect me to believe that?" asked the sheriff.

"That is what he did," responded Mr Smith, then added: "He never exactly told them to go on."

"Did you protest?" challenged Sheriff Dudley.

"I could not very well protest when he allowed them to go on again," came the response.

Dismissing the driver's version as "nonsense", the sheriff found the case proven and the accused were fined £1.

Of course while buses may fulfil a public need they are also a business, and packing passengers in equates to profit.

Having someone nick your fares though is likely to bring a red mist down over the timetable and two rival bus companies on the same route was a ticket for trouble which, in July 1927, landed driver Walter Edwin Price, of Nether Street, Dysart, in the dock at Cupar.

He was charged with ramming into another bus near Burntisland war memorial on Kinghorn Road after he thought it was picking up his rightful passengers. The other driver, David

Adamson Glendinning, Rossland Place, Kinghorn, protested his innocence and that Mr Price had recklessly cut into the halt at the memorial.

The result was that Mr Glendinning's bus was forced on to the footpath by the force of the collision, though Mr Price, supported by his conductress, claimed there had been no contact at all between the two vehicles – testimony to the sturdiness of their construction since it apparently could not be confirmed contact had actually occurred.

According to a report of the case in the Fife Free Press & Kirkcaldy Guardian, Sheriff Dudley Stuart said that if there had been no contact then Mr Price would not be standing before him and it would have been likely the two drivers would merely have exchanged "complimentary epithets" at the scene, though one would imagine a colourful use of language was probably employed anyhow.

Imposing a fine of 40 shillings and seven days to pay, with the option of 10 days in jail, the sheriff warned against any repeat of such bus stop bedlam.

Sheriff Stuart issued a warning to bus drivers and, according to the newspaper, "wished to make clear that if more of these cases arose out of rivalry, which involved danger to the public, he would deal heavily with them. He hoped all other drivers would take a warning".

That wasn't the only bus incident Sheriff Stuart had to deal with on that particular sitting. There was another intriguing case though the newspapers failed to elaborate on the background.

The case involved an East Neuk conductress who collected a 10 shilling fine for driving a bus without a licence. As to whether she just fancied a birl while the driver stretched his legs, was given a shot at the wheel or spotted a passenger and used her initiative before a rival bus came along, we will never know.

Of course the local newspapers of the past regularly carried reports of the mishaps that befell the bus services that rumbled through the streets from dawn until dark.

Unlike the train and the tram, the omnibus was propelled by the internal combustion engine, and the word combustion offers a clue to one of the major hazards – fire.

It seems the East Neuk had a particular grievance over the condition of the vehicles serving the communities from a bus back-firing in August 1930, which subsequently did exactly that, go on fire at the back. Fortunately there were no passengers on board and the driver on the St Andrews to Dunino route managed to douse the flames but not before much damage was caused.

So in an era of busy buses with the occasional tendency to ignite, it would seem a major tragedy was always possible just around the next bend.

In fact, in September 1938, Fife came very close to suffering a horror that would have been forever etched into its history had it not been for the quick-thinking and heroic actions of Andrew Bloomfield.

The 51-year-old Dysart man was first on the scene when a full double-decker bus crashed near his home and caught fire.

Mr Bloomfield, a garage proprietor of No 28 Holding on the main Kirkcaldy to East Wemyss road, sprang into action and, as a result, into the headlines, extra colour being added by the fact that our hero only had one arm.

The bus, packed across the two decks with factory girls and working men travelling from Buckhaven through the Wemyss to Kirkcaldy, was being driven by James Johnston, 18 Aitken Street, Prinlaws, Leslie, when it suffered a blow out around 7.30am. The burst tyre forced the bus out of control and it ploughed into a telegraph pole, through a low wall then keeled over on to its side.

The crash saw the bus come to rest with the passenger entrance to the ground, trapping everyone inside with no means of escape.

Mr Bloomfield at that moment was having breakfast with his family and raced to the scene of the accident. As chaos reigned inside the bus, he kicked in several of the windows and started to help the passengers out when flames began to lick out from beneath the cabin.

The screams from the trapped passengers alerted folk on the nearby small holdings and they rushed to join in the rescue. Mr Bloomfield realised they couldn't get everyone free in time and raced to the garage next to his house, grabbed a fire extinguisher and returned to the bus to tackle the flames. The driver managed to kick out his windscreen and Mr Bloomfield fought the blaze while the remaining passengers escaped to safety. Those injured were taken to his house for attention.

"The place was like a hospital," Mrs Bloomfield told the Leven Advertiser & Wemyss Gazette.

Her husband's efforts to save the vehicle looked to be in vain when the extinguisher ran out and the flames again took hold. But just then another bus arrived on the scene and its on-board extinguisher was used to kill the fire.

A nightmarish tragedy was averted and just four passengers required hospital treatment with only one detained, 16-year-old Georgina Smart, 26 Lochhead Road, Coaltown of Wemyss, who sustained head and leg injuries.

Three others were treated for shock – Elizabeth Wilson (14), 54 Forth Street; Mary Waiters (14), 5 Swan Street, and Mary Snaddon, 42 Forth Street, all Denbeath, and all employed in the Kirkcaldy factory of the Boase Spinning Company.

"It was a dreadful experience," one of the girls told the Leven Advertiser. "I heard the explosion of the tyre then, suddenly, there was a terrific lurch which sent me spinning into the gangway.

"The next thing I knew was that we seemed to be piled on each other against the windows. Then, to make matters worse, we saw flames shooting from the front of the bus."

Another said: "The passengers became a kicking, struggling mass ... if it hadn't been for the promptitude of the rescuers we might all have been burnt."

Unfortunately the hazards of fire persisted and there was another lucky escape in January 1948 when a bus carrying workers from Methil and Leven to Crail aerodrome went on fire.

The blaze started under the floor and it was with some difficulty that the burning chassis was brought under control. The bus limped along to Elie when fire broke out again, but this time a garage was able to assist.

"The accident brought to a head complaints by workers about the old buses taking them to work, and a deputation was appointed to protest to the bus company," reported the Dundee Evening Telegraph.

Courting trouble
and capturing readers

The court case has always been compulsive reading in a local newspaper. It combines nosiness into untoward behaviour with, hopefully, at least a passing recognition of the offender. On a national level voyeurism has to take over with the salacious, gory or grotesque capturing the reader but, locally, the offence is magnified by the gossip factor.

These tales have populated the pages for over a century as publishers ensured a shorthand note in the court equated to sales of the title. There are a number of journalists who believe the days of print could well have remained healthy if their proprietors had retained a commitment to covering the wrongdoings within our communities. Instead, this has been allowed to slip and, perhaps more importantly, that philosophy of justice not only being done but being seen to be done has all but disappeared, certainly on a local level.

Of course, plundering these cases from more recent times in a publication such as this brings with it a legal hazard. Despite being in the public domain, minor or summary cases will more often than not mean a spent conviction and resurrecting them for entertainment or titillation opens the doors to defamation.

But, since reputation is personal, the deceased cannot be offended, and historic trawls through the archives produce fascinating insights into incidents that once would have set tongues wagging.

Time though hasn't really changed the bulk of those offences. Drunkenness, assaults, breaches of the peace, theft and the like seem to be a permanent part of human behaviour, but there are also occasions when the baffling, bizarre and bewildering make the headlines.

Recounting these though isn't always without protest. Not so long ago a Facebook page saw a post regarding a 1916 case concerning a prominent name from St Monans' heritage.

Now this wasn't a curtain-twitching incident but an offence that offered an insight into a part of our social history — on a daily and dairy basis ... margarine.

At the heart of it was James Miller, a senior partner in the firm of Messrs Miller & Thomson, the foundation of the renowned Miller's boatbuilding business.

Back in 1916 Miller & Thomson also operated as a grocer and Mr Miller found himself before the court in Cupar pleading guilty to two charges under the Margarine Act.

And Mr Miller's 'crime' was one of typography.

Though it is long forgotten now, the spread of margarine, a more affordable alternative to butter, churned up a bit of trouble. Basically, the butter bosses needed to protect their product so a number of rules and regulations were passed, and it was these Mr Miller's business contravened.

The Dundee Evening Telegraph reported that Miller & Thomson had been able to balance the grocery trade with its other operation – boat building and ship chandlery. The outbreak of war had seen the firm take on a greater amount of work for the Admiralty, building a large number of motor launches.

So while Mr Miller's focus was primarily on helping the war effort, the management of the shop was handed over to a member of staff. Unfortunately, on her watch, a packet of margarine was delivered in a wrapper where the word margarine was not printed in letters greater than half an inch long; and the second charge was selling margarine without the right size of label.

Given the Great War was raging, lives were being lost by the thousands every day, it seems astonishing that the powers-that-be in Fife saw fit to charge a man helping his country with the offence of permitting the use of an incorrect point size on the typeface used for his margarine labels.

Mr Miller was fined £1 for each offence with another £1 towards expenses. The alternative was 10 days imprisonment.

Now here was a case that surely had to be of interest, both locally and wider afield? In its own way this didn't just capture a piece of local history but also highlighted what priorities remained on the home front while the carnage on Western Front continued unabated.

Unfortunately, it wasn't seen that way in present day St Monans. The Facebook post was deemed offensive and promptly removed. As to whether the complaints emanated from the descendants of the Miller family who felt a lingering shame over the margarine typography case a century ago or, perhaps, from the descendants of the jobsworths who brought the case remains unknown.

So, perhaps it is best to avoid closed communities where descendants remain tetchy down the decades, or keep to names common enough where present day links are so diluted that connections are hard to establish.

And that brings us to one court case that is fascinating on so many levels. First, there is the apparent sudden inexplicable behaviour of the offender. Of course there is no attempt here to mitigate his unlawful actions but it can be argued they, with the passage of time, were entirely linked and, perhaps, motivated by the greed and opportunism of his neighbours. While the celebration of a criminal is not the intention, as far as Fife's Forgotten Tales go, the so-called 'Jeremy Diddler' deserves his place in our folklore.

We are unsure where his story begins, possibly it was rooted late in 1869 but it blossomed forth in the early months of 1870.

The Fifeshire Advertiser pulled the strands of the tale together in May of that year with the 'Jeremy Diddler' making his appearance in the news columns for Markinch. The diddler's real name was David 'Davie' Ritchie of that parish, a retired labourer and, from what we can establish, a regular and unremarkable resident.

For some inexplicable reason Davie let it be broadcast that he'd had a brother who, some 30 years previous, had ventured abroad to seek his fortune, settling in Madras in the state of Tamil Nadu, India. The brothers hadn't kept in touch but word had arrived from that far flung colony that his brother had died and left Davie, his sole heir, with a tidy sum of £9000, which converts into today's money as £1,062,400 – a fair-sized nest egg for retirement in Markinch.

"The story got wind," reported the Fifeshire Advertiser, "and Davie's company was courted by those who knew nothing of his existence before.

"The favours that follow Mammon surrounded him; and publicans, grocers, tailors, drapers, shoemakers and bakers, all displayed a readiness to have Davie (now Mr) Ritchie as one of their customers."

Accounts were opened for him, cash was freely lent and, although no documentation was ever shown confirming his newly-inherited wealth, Davie's credit was good, and not just locally.

He took to venturing further afield, his reputation preceding him. According to the Advertiser one publican in Balgonie provided a brief note of introduction to an innkeeper in Edinburgh which simply stated: "This is David Ritchie. Be kind to David." No doubt a tab and a tap were duly opened.

Although now in the autumn of his years, the Madras windfall didn't just make him welcome at many a hearth but proved capable of melting at least one heart. From Markinch he journeyed to the Lang Toun where he became entangled with a "fair dame", apparently abandoning her as he neared the point where a breach of promise could be levelled at him, and the expenses that would inevitably incur.

"It is said he dressed her gorgeously, at the expense of somebody, from a draper's shelves in Kirkcaldy," continued the Advertiser.

However, a day of financial reckoning was ahead, with Davie doing his best to put off the visit he said he had with a solicitor in Cupar that would see the transfer of his fortune from South Asia. His reluctance to keep this appointment raised suspicion and concern among his new-found fair-weather friends and the result was he upped sticks from Markinch and took to the road, along with his tall tale.

According to the newspapers, he enjoyed spells in Auchtermuchty, Strathmiglo, Newburgh, Dunfermline and Dundee, but word was out and, in the first week of May 1870, he was apprehended at Thornton station. In his company were two men, one who had lent him 30 shillings and the other who had pawned his watch to help Davie travel to his lawyer's offices in Cupar. Whatever you think of him, there can be little doubt that Davie definitely had been blessed with the gift of the gab.

So the next stop for the 'Jeremy Diddler' was the solicitor, and this appointment marked the end of the line for his inheritance caper.

Statements were subsequently taken, mainly from Markinch, and on Tuesday, May 17, 1870, Davie appeared before sheriff and jury at Cupar. The charges, stretching from early January, covered falsehood, fraud and wilful imposition.

Given his well chronicled spree there was just a handful of charges, covering loans, clothes and boots. He pleaded guilty on all counts and was jailed for six months. There would appear to be an absence of information as to his situation on release but one would imagine a return to Markinch might have been uncomfortable.

Horror and sorrow
at triple tragedy

While the press, particularly in the form of local newspapers, offers an insight into community life, that is but a snapshot, often just those "15 minutes of fame" – or notoriety – before those featured fade into history.

The longer versions of those individual contributions to that life, unless earnestly researched and chronicled, are lost beneath headstone inscriptions and the grave doesn't surrender those tales.

There are occasions where the time that binds life and death together is brief; where the cemetery can yield very little to what is known, and such short stories are always the case with the young.

Family is the security for a child. No matter how dysfunctional, warped and fragile that relationship may be, if it is all that has been experienced, then it is the norm. But in those cases where parents kill those who look to them for protection, there isn't a commonality of deviance.

The double child murders in Leven by Andrew Clark in 1930 were, of course, horrific and while there is nothing that could, or should, be said in mitigation of his atrocious acts, here was a man broken by hardship and misfortune. It would be hoped that from this tragedy lessons would be learned that such desperation and despair would always, in future, be identified and addressed with support. Some progress has been made, but it could be argued, not nearly enough.

Reports from the time indicate, while revulsion and outrage would have been present, the community mood that prevailed was more one of sorrow, perhaps made heavier by the realisation that the distance between what is perceived as a 'normal' happy life and hopelessness can be very short.

His funeral, and that of his daughters, on Saturday, June 14, 1930, saw a massive turnout, access restricted to Scoonie cemetery and news reports filed across the country. But until shortly after 10am on the Thursday, just two days before, few people had heard of him.

While 40-year-old Clark's journey to national notoriety really only began on that Wednesday, his journey to despair had been much longer, and the conclusion of his life was the opening chapter of a story that captured national attention.

News quickly spread on that Thursday morning that a man had been struck and killed on the train line crossing Leven Links. He had been spotted walking the embankment on the course, failed to respond to any acknowledgements and took up a position by a hut on Cattle Creep on the 10th hole. As the 10am Anstruther to Glasgow train approached, he removed his boots and leapt in front of the engine.

Witnessing the act, greenkeepers and golfers raced to the scene and the horribly mutilated body. Despite the injuries, the victim was recognised and identified as Andrew Clark, well-kent in the local golfing community as he often worked as a caddie.

The police and, as a formality, a doctor were summoned, and Clark's body was removed to the mortuary at Scoonie.

It was known the dead man, who was a widower, lived at Triangle Place in South Street, Leven, very much an old part of the town, wedged in that area between Buchlyvie Terrace and Henderson Street, near the Shorehead. He lived with his daughter, Jean (10), and step-daughter Bella Campbell (17), and the next stage was to inform them of the death of their father, but the girls were nowhere to be found.

Neighbours reported there had already been two visitors that morning, the first, an insurance collector, and the second, the school attendance officer who, being unable to get an answer, had asked if the family were away from home. Although no-one had seen them, it was reckoned Bella would be inside, but just sleeping late.

This raised concern and the door was eventually forced.

"We found ourselves in the kitchen, and at first saw nothing unusual," a neighbour told the Fife Free Press & Kirkcaldy Guardian. "Then we noticed Jean lying on the bed with the bedclothes over her mouth. She was dead.

"Bella was not to be seen, so I opened the room door but there was no sign of her there. I lifted the valance of the bed and there she was, lying stiff and cold.

"It was an awful experience. I could not cry, but I will never forget it as long as I live."

The police then had the task of trying to piece together exactly what drove an apparently upstanding man, who seemed to get on well with his daughters, to kill them both and then take his own life.

According to the newspaper reports syndicated at the time, it soon became known he was one of the 'Old Contemptibles', a member of the Black Watch who served with the 1914 Expeditionary Force. He had been wounded but returned to the front line, serving until 1918. Then, on being demobbed, he returned home, finding work down Leven pit which lay in the Kirkland area, between Methilhaven and Wellesley Roads.

He'd married 10 years previously, raising Bella as his own with the couple going on to have Jean.

His wife had died three years before and his grief had never subsided while he endeavoured to cope as a single parent.

Changes at the pit saw him unemployed and he struggled to find work. However, his knowledge of golf saw him earn some money as a caddie. The previous month he had caddied at the Amateur Open at St Andrews when the legendary Bobby Jones won the title in front of a crowd of 15,000.

And, just the week before Clark took his life, he and a friend set out to walk to the Royal Liverpool Golf Club in Hoylake, England, in the hope of picking up some more caddying work at the Open Championship. The pair took the wrong route though, finding themselves on the east coast rather than the west, and were forced to wend a weary way back home to Fife.

So, out of work and out of luck, the hardship the single dad was facing was evident, but that didn't help the police explain his killing his daughters. However, a Bible on the table clarified that mystery as, between the pages, lay Clark's handwritten confession, penned after the death of Bella and while waiting for Jean to return home.

It would seem Clark quarrelled over money with Bella, who had recently started work as an attendant at the Beach Concert Hall in Leven, in the early afternoon of the Wednesday. In the heat of the row the step-daughter had struck Clark with her shoe. In a rage he grabbed her and killed her through strangulation, then hid the body under the bed in the front room.

Realising the vileness of his deed, and without clarity of thought, he felt it impossible for Jean to be branded in life as the daughter of a murderer and resolved to kill her too then take his own life. Jean came home and, after her tea, her father allowed her to go out to play.

It is impossible to imagine what turmoil was going on in Clark's thoughts through the next hours. He ventured outdoors and met with an acquaintance, telling him: "This is the worst nicht I've ever put in. It's been that long." He also checked with a neighbour the times of the trains in the morning.

It would seem when Jean returned home and went to bed, her father waited until she was asleep then suffocated her with a pillow.

The desolation in that house in South Street as a father sat with his two dead daughters is unimaginable and his confession concluded with a request that the two girls be buried beside their mother and the comment: "If their mother had lived this would never have happened."

At 9am on the Thursday morning he headed to the Labour Exchange to sign on, and then began his walk towards Leven Links and his chosen point on the railway line.

Silent crowds lined the streets for the funeral on the Saturday. Clark's body had been removed from the mortuary earlier and already lay beside the family plot as the two white coffins, lying side by side in the hearse, made their way to Scoonie cemetery where admission was restricted to the cortege.

The Scotsman reported that, after a brief graveside service, Clark's coffin was lowered first, followed by Bella then Jean.

The hole truth
and nothing but the truth

For all its tragedy, the Clark case weaves together two aspects of life in old Fife – mining and golf. While the sport is now a global phenomenon and, in many countries, an exclusive pursuit, the Kingdom's municipal courses put the game within everyone's reach. The hardship of a working life underground and the often blustery challenges of the links were not mutually exclusive.

Times have changed for the pits as well as the pitch and putt. The collieries have all gone and the tees forced to compete for fees, though Fife Golf Trust is to be commended for keeping access to the community greens as wide as possible.

That is how it should be, given Fife lays claim to possessing the Home of Golf and The Open, when it returns to St Andrews, commands world interest and respect.

Of course the journey towards the presentation of the Claret Jug doesn't begin with the first starting time. That really is the final stage after months, and now years, of preparation and organisation. The international audience has little interest in the minutiae of detail before the tournament proper, but it can be of major significance to the local community.

Given the first Open in St Andrews was in 1873, the Fife local newspapers have chronicled its growth and development, particularly well placed being the St Andrews Citizen. The tens of thousands of words written don't just focus on the winners and the glorious losers, but the entire social history that has evolved alongside the tournament. It is a unique record, invaluable, and largely forgotten or ignored by Fifers.

Johnston Press, which at that time owned the Fife Free Press Group, attempted to remedy that by utilising its archive to mark the championship's 29th return to the Old Course in 2015.

The idea was to produce a commemorative publication built around extracts from the company portfolio that would chart the local perspective of The Open over a century in a traditional turn of the century newspaper format.

Editorially it was a challenging project, though a successful one. Commercially, however, the real test for such an enterprise, it was disappointing. Although some sponsorship was secured, very few Fife advertisers saw a return for participating and that, coupled with logistical distribution difficulties, led to a very limited circulation during the Championship.

Some enterprising individuals did later post the publication on eBay but the ultimate ignominy came when, faced with pulping numerous bundles, the British Golf Museum was offered them free of charge but declined to take them.

As a result this rare, historic 'Celebration' had a limited readership and life, though it is always possible a revival and update may make it a viable project for a future return of The Open to the Home of Golf.

Of special interest in the publication were a number of articles drawn from the St Andrews Citizen during the 1930s that marked the retirement from the game of those who had helped shape the sport. While the grainy photographs and the names wouldn't spark instant recognition among readers, their tales not only covered their ambassadorships for the sport but here were the men who actually knew, worked with, played against or caddied for legends.

There was Willie Auchterlonie who won the Championship at Prestwick in 1893 at the age of 21. He was praised as a young professional for wresting the title away from the amateurs who were dominating the game.

"His play all through was remarkable for its steadiness," wrote the Yorkshire Post & Leeds Intelligencer after his victory. "He is a strong young fellow and playing all the departments of the game equally well."

Auchterlonie made the headlines in the St Andrews Citizen in September 1935 when, at the age of 62, he was appointed the professional at the Royal and Ancient Golf Club.

A particularly colourful character was interviewed in January 1937. David Cuthbert was a professional, taught alongside Tom Morris, helped develop the game in America, caddied for the great Harry Vardon, then returned to caddy in St Andrews.

Cuthbert really had done just about all there was to do in the game, and he had strong views as well, particularly on the expanding range of clubs now permitted for golfers.

"It's no gowf at a' they play nooadays," he told the Citizen. "It's a fu' swing every time wi' a different club and that canna be ca'd gowf.

"Good old gowfers could play better gowf wi' one club than some can noo wi' eight clubs."

June that year saw the passing of 71-year-old George McIntyre, St Andrews' oldest caddie. In the Citizen's obituary, it is recorded that he first picked up a bag at the age of 11. Over the next 60 years his knowledge of the game and the Old Course was second to none. Not only had this Fifer seen the game, and the famous course, as well as St Andrews town itself, evolve, he also personally knew Old Tom Morris and young Tommy, saying of the latter: "He was, in his day and generation, one of the finest golfers that ever handled a club."

Sharing his memories in the Citizen in 1938 was Walter Anderson, a contemporary of Open winners Sandy Herd and James Braid. Anderson chose to make clubs rather than swing them but, in his younger days, he could hold his own with the best.

"As a boy he witnessed many of the famous money matches, and later was to figure in some himself," reported the Citizen.

Mourning the advent of the steel shafted club, Anderson still made his own wooden clubs and at 69 played two rounds a week with his peers, delivering a "sound game".

There will be many more of golf's great characters waiting to be rediscovered in the archives of the St Andrews Citizen and its sister paper the Fife Herald. If you consider the wordage generated by the millionaire players on the circuit today, and Fife's proud claim as 'Home of Golf', it is sad the winners have their place in history but those Fifers who laid the foundation stones for the modern game are, in many cases, all but lost.

Of course while these characters could recall the evolution of the game, most were St Andrews born and bred and were witness to the changes in the town.

As George McIntyre said: "St Andrews was a delightful place to live in the old days. There was a quietness in the city then that has almost entirely gone with the coming of the motor car."

The explosion in the game as a spectator sport also effected changes on St Andrews. New hotels opened and, particularly during The Open, the demand for accommodation far outstripped supply.

"The demand is extending all down the coast, and reports from Anstruther, Crail, Pittenweem, St Monans and Elie show that they are well booked up also," said the Citizen in April 1946. "Prices being charged in first class hotels vary from one guinea to five guineas per day for full board and lodgings."

That's a problem that hasn't been solved through the decades though the local newspapers record the efforts being made to accommodate this influx, from floating accommodation to extending car parks for the flood of visitors. And, of course, the changes to the tournament itself are all recorded – the first bookmakers being allowed, the crowd control measures, the first television cameras, even the first helicopter.

The Open remains a logistical and sporting phenomenon today and St Andrews has been a part of that since the 19th century.

The Championship's connection with the town is still being written and the 30 previous chapters featuring the famous links are a fascinating part of Fife history.

Matters of the heart
and convenience

Given the "Who, What, Where, Why, When?" mantra of the reporter's world, these questions are often dealt with at the most basic levels as editors balance the flow of news with the space available within the journal's columns.

As a result, many a tale begs further research to flesh out the narrative behind the published details but this may involve an expedition where an arduous journey results in a disappointing destination.

The articles herein invite those so-inclined readers of Forgotten Fife Tales to pursue a fuller and better framed picture but while the scribes and hacks of the past were happy, and of course entitled, to publish the names and addresses of those entangled with the Establishment and authority, entanglements of the heart were an entirely different matter. There, it would seem, it was often deemed best to spare the names and spare the blushes.

Of course these cases, in their day, would have been familiar to those in immediate proximity to their unfolding but without the actual specifics of those involved the broadcasting of them would ensure privacy while still providing some titillation. No doubt, that vagueness, combined perhaps with embellishment, would dilute the story to such an extent that any legal offices acting on behalf of those taking offence would be aware that proceedings would widen embarrassment and spread blushes further afield.

Two such cases are worth recounting here and those with an investigative nature may well consider it worthwhile to seek to furnish more defined details; those with a more creative leaning will take them as they are – good yarns.

The first was deemed notable in that the tale involved the high and mighty.

The Sportsman publication in December 1866 summed it up thus: "Amidst all the 'gag' that one hears a little too much of nowadays about the seduction of marvellously innocent girls by horrible dogcart-driving sinners of men, under the most disadvantageous circumstances, it is now and then a change to find that the boy is sometimes run away with the girl."

Aside from the gossip columns of newspapers and magazines up and down the country, perhaps this tale is well-recorded in a dusty journal sealed and secreted away in a desk or cupboard down a dark corridor in that most noble of establishments, the political power generator that is Eton College, Windsor, for it was an 'old boy' who became one of the two central characters.

What gave this tale its 'juice' though, was the other character and, from an era where class and sexism were facts of life, she was from 'downstairs' and, according to the report, "buxom" as well.

The mileage in this racy story is underlined by the fact that a full report even appeared in the North Devon Journal, a location quite some distance removed from Fife, proving good gossip can always defy expected geographical boundaries.

To set the scene for its readers, the Journal immediately tackled that newspaper mantra with an attention-grabbing summation where the key elements can be broken down as:

(Who?) The eldest son of a prominent family and his father's cook.

(What?) Elopement.

(Where?) Fifeshire.

(Why?) Boy meets buxom woman.

(When?) Recently.

In truth, there's enough there to piece together the story for yourself but let's add some colour.

According to the North Devon Journal's Scotland-based correspondent, the young gentleman, groomed for greatness, had not long returned from the cloisters of Eton where he had harvested an impressive crop of academic honours.

His life's path seemed prepared for him: nurtured, cultivated and now educated, the next step would be a suitable marriage and a "young and beautiful" heiress was apparently waiting in the wings, and expecting to step from there into the church aisle.

But this version of the anticipated story would not conclude with the traditional "and they lived happily ever after" as the cast was joined by what the Journal described as a "buxom brunette … some years older than the bridegroom, and has been in the family for a considerable period".

We are informed this older woman was the cook for the master of the house and presume the relationship with the young Etonian was not approved of upstairs.

So, it would seem literally, if you can't stand the heat, get out of the kitchen, and the pair eloped, making for a love nest in the Angus harbour town of Montrose.

"The father of the hero followed," reported the Journal, "but only to find them slumbering in each other's arms."

36

The Sportsman set a slightly more dramatic image: "Thither the angry father – without, it seems, the conventional 'brace of pistols under his arm' of ancient minstrelsy – followed, and, at the witching hour of night, found the pair happily asleep together."

Now the tale to this point is very much gentry meets commoner and results in shame. We know little about the servant lass other than her hair colour, figure ... and that she can cook.

The concluding part of the Journal's report, brief though it is, tells us much more about her character and perhaps explains why our young man had his head turned from a pretty heiress.

So ... the fuming father did not take finding the couple entwined too well, and the report continues:

"So enraged was the old gentleman that, forgetting all delicacy, he was about to eject her from the bedroom, when she collared her quondum {former} master and hurled him headlong from the apartment.

"The runaway son endeavoured to explain and pacify his insulted parent when the lady seized her husband, and, conveying him almost vi et armis {by force and arms} back to the bedroom, locked the door."

We are told in conclusion that the couple married and honeymooned in Gloucestershire, where the parents of the bride kept a small "public and grocery".

Closing the Journal's archive on this particular tale does ignite an interest into what happened next but, like all good stories, more detail may dilute the flavour. After all, too many cooks ...

Our next tale, while perhaps a match at least locally for gossip value, could not be further removed from the essence of the former.

Here is not an incident of passion, but of planning; where recklessness is controlled by caution; where the heart is stilled by the head; and where, it should always be remembered, the railroad track into a town is the same track out of it.

This time we do have an exact location, that being Cupar, though names are again withheld. The year is 1876, just a decade after the elopement, and given the tight-knit community that Cupar was, and is, one would assume the main character involved in this incident would certainly be well-kent, and even more so after its conclusion.

Again, the report circulated beyond Fife with the Dundee Advertiser and Glasgow Herald sharing the tale with its readers. At one time the aim of those whose business was to populate the news-stands was to inform, educate and entertain; this would certainly fulfil at least one of those lofty ambitions.

The event that set the typewriters clicking occurred on Saturday, June 3, 1876, and was a wedding, or, to be precise, the absence of one.

Scheduled for 10am that summer morning, matrimonial proceedings had been arranged quickly and by special licence. Again, the anticipated "and they lived happily ever after" ending did not go entirely to script with the couple quite dramatically and suddenly 'uncoupling'.

Our central character, and he does indeed appear to be a character, was a well-known bachelor. Marriage had by all accounts appealed to him but the art of courtship was beyond him, as was one-to-one communication.

Pursuit of his perfect partner had been through advertisements in the "lonely hearts" columns of the day with such correspondence offering a greater degree of control and consideration.

One would expect to see the 19th century equivalent of "GSOH required" from our bachelor and, indeed, his requirements would seem to have required that sense of humour as a very healthy bank balance was one of his first priorities for anyone wishing to share his life in the Howe of Fife. The requirement was that she had a £3000 bank balance in her name. Converting that to 2020 figures, it was the equivalent of insisting any possible paramour should possess a purse bulging with around £340,000.

There were no takers.

Instead a new approach seems to have been taken with him responding to other advertisers. A connection was finally made when he responded to one lady who was seeking a position as a housekeeper to a single gentleman.

There is no easily accessible record of his approach but it appears he confirmed that he did indeed require a housekeeper but preferred if that role could come attached to a wider remit, that of wife.

Although a reluctant communicator in the face-to-face tradition, it would seem the bachelor had a way with the written word.

The quality of his quill-work was such that a regular correspondence developed and, according to the Glasgow Herald, this flourished into "gushing love epistles" with the correspondents becoming increasingly enamoured with one another.

Unfortunately, we never learn exactly from whence this lady friend hailed but we are told, on it being agreed she should venture to Fife, that she asked for £5 to cover her expenses.

His response is intriguing. Either he was frugal or romantic, because he only provided half of that, £2 10s. You could argue the former in that he perhaps checked ticket prices and the cheapest lodgings, or, in the latter case, the £5 was for a return journey, one that would not be required as love would bind them forever together in Cupar.

At this point we should give him the benefit of the doubt. He arranged to meet his intended in Edinburgh on the Tuesday, brought her across to Cupar and took rooms for her in a hotel on the Wednesday.

Then, through Thursday and Friday, they strolled through the town. He introducing her as his prospective wife with she, reportedly, describing him as "such a jewel".

The minister was duly cornered with a request being made for a speedy wedding. The fact that a church ceremony wasn't possible until the good lady had been resident in the parish for six weeks meant alternative plans had to be quickly made.

So a special licence was obtained and the time for the marriage set at 10am in a hotel on the Saturday. Come the hour, the bride, a sheriff officer and witnesses assembled but, by 10.15, there was still no sign of the groom.

One can imagine the tension mounting and the growing concern, and humiliation, the bride must have felt. Eventually in exasperation and anger she departed the hotel and made her way to her husband-to-be's home to demand an explanation for his absence. His response was that he had slept in, but he didn't appear to be in too much of a hurry to take his vows.

"When they reached the hotel the bachelor had apparently made up his mind that single happiness was preferable to what was now appearing to him as dubious double blessedness," reported the Glasgow Herald.

"The gay deceiver is said to have come gradually to this conclusion after comparing the carte with the original in the most favourable light.

"A scene then ensued, but the bachelor remained obdurate to the entreaties, the expostulations, and the threats of his would-be wife."

The ruction wasn't settled in a secluded environment. Instead, it was reported they walked the streets of Cupar, no doubt in some form of negotiation, and come the evening that return ticket was needed with the jilted bride catching the 7.40pm train to London.

"It is understood the matter has been settled by a money arrangement," reported the Dundee Advertiser.

As to the final marital fate of the two main protagonists that may remain buried under less dramatic headlines with no reference made to the cold feet in Cupar incident.

'A case of common brutality unrelieved by any romance'

There are certain ugly historical events that, despite their drama and public lure, we would prefer to erase from memory. Such editing though can be viewed as denial and the fact that a researcher, writer or reader can still be fascinated and shocked today perhaps underlines a lasting human weakness to witness the grotesque and grisly.

And so it is with the execution of the Scanlan brothers in 1852, an event that saw all roads lead to Fife to observe death by judicial decree. Sixteen years later in Dumfries, 19-year-old Robert Smith, guilty of rape and murder, would become the last person to be publicly hanged in Scotland. It was estimated approximately 600 gathered to view the teenager's death and repulsion at the hanging reportedly saw many turn their backs and some even flee the scene.

The Cupar hanging was entirely different. Thousands, many from outwith the Kingdom, journeyed to the county town. The number of spectators shocked the local press but interest was national and reports of the final hours of the Irish brothers appeared in newspapers from John O'Groats to the Home Counties.

The Cupar-based Fife Herald, with the Fluthers market site of the scaffold on its doorstep, provided extensive coverage, just as it had of the trial. Yet, despite the many thousands of words filed across Britain on the crime and the punishment, the execution on the morning of Monday, July 5, of Michael and Peter Scanlan has become one of Fife's forgotten tales.

While the condemned men are the centre of this story, they are, and always should be, secondary to Margaret Maxwell Hilton, an elderly woman who sold meal and bread to labourers, and whose murder was callous and brutal. She deserves her place in the brightness beyond the shadows of the scaffold and to be remembered as a poor, innocent and frightened victim.

Although the legal arguments at the trial were long and protracted the bare facts of the case were simple. Margaret, who stayed in the hamlet of Hilton of Forthar, in the parish of Kettle, was at home on the evening of Sunday, February 15, 1852, when the back window of her house was broken and intruders entered.

41

In the robbery that followed, Margaret was beaten to death with a heavy wooden stool. Suspicion quickly fell on Michael and Peter Scanlan, aged approximately 25 and 22 respectively, who lodged next door to her and had quarrelled with her while settling a bill. A third man, found with a stolen watch from the house, said he had been the lookout at the robbery and his testimony at the High Court in Edinburgh was crucial. At the conclusion of the trial on June 14, the brothers were sentenced to death on charges of murder, stouthreif {threat of violence} and theft.

In the aftermath of the sentence being carried out, the Fife Herald asserted: "It was a case of common brutality unrelieved by any romance.

"To those who are fascinated by what is tragic, and take an interest in seeing poor human nature in the 'hour and power of darkness', this murder possessed no features but those of harsh and unmitigated ruffianism. The thread of the crime was as common and repulsive as the rope which punished it. It was simply and exclusively horrible."

But the Herald did acknowledge there were three circumstances which did give this particular crime additional interest in Fife and acted as a powerful magnet for the crowds.

To start with there hadn't been a murder in Fife for 20 years or an execution for 22. Secondly there was the peculiarity that the perpetrators of the deed had been brothers and, finally, the fact that, from when they were first apprehended, the Scanlans had steadfastly declared their innocence. Although this was expressed with some vehemence at their sentencing, they had remained calm prior and thereafter with this apparent coolness seen as evidence that they believed they would be vindicated. They repeatedly said that God knew them to perfectly innocent, and that as soon as Margaret Maxwell saw them, she would declare: "You are not the boys that murdered me."

Although that resolve and composure remained constant, it failed to convince the public of their innocence.

"Owing to the absence of any extenuating circumstances attending the crime, there was no effort made on the part of the public in general to obtain a modification of the punishment," reported the Lancaster Gazette.

"Two petitions were indeed got up in Cupar on behalf of the younger brother, but comparatively few signatures were attached to either of them, and little hope was entertained of any favourable answer."

And none came.

Groups of people began to assemble around the enclosure of the scaffold from sunset on the Sunday and, as dawn broke on the Monday of the execution, Cupar's streets were already filling up.

The Dundee, Perth & Cupar Advertiser reported: "Early in the morning there was every appearance of a beautiful and warm day, and vast multitudes flocked from the adjacent country on foot to gratify their morbid curiosity, by gazing at two fellow creatures suffering the most ignominious death the law can inflict.

"A large number were from the direction of Kirkforthar, where the murder was committed, while extra trains were run from Dunfermline, and from Burntisland, the latter probably bringing passengers from Edinburgh as the ordinary trains would not have arrived until the appalling occurrence was almost wholly finished.

"The consequence of this crowding to Cupar was that, long before the hour of execution, a large concourse of spectators was assembled in the vicinity of the gallows. The majority of the spectators were not women, and altogether the crowd was not of that repugnant character usual at such scenes in large towns. No ribald conversation was carried on, nor barbarous and brutal jests perpetrated, as is generally the case in executions."

That, however, would change, much to the disgust of at least one local paper which led it to publish a scathing condemnation of this multitude of voyeurs.

As the village green drew crowds from all directions, others settled for a more distant view while the roofs and windows of nearby houses also provided much sought-after viewing points. Reports syndicated from correspondents at the scene estimated the turnout to be as great as 12,000.

That number was swelled by extra security measures introduced when reports were received that a large number of Irish workmen in Dundee had resolved to disrupt the execution and, perhaps, even stage a rescue. As a result, the newspapers said approximately 40 of the 7th Hussars from Jock's Lodge, Edinburgh, were despatched to Cupar, and 60 or so members of the 42nd Regiment of Foot (Highlanders) journeyed from Dundee and took up position at the jail.

In addition to that military presence, around the area of the scaffold there were 35 police officers, 180 special constables from the burgh and 100 from the surrounding areas.

The gallows, on loan from Edinburgh, had been erected during the night on the Fluthers, within a few feet of the north-east limit of the boundary of the burgh, close to the houses on Braehead. Its assembly meant the hammer blows echoed through the stillness of the small hours and would have been clearly heard in the cells of the condemned men. The construction of the gibbet for their final seconds of life would add to an earlier trauma. Having heard, although this was false, that the executed were handed over for medical dissection, the brothers sought, and received, assurances their bodies would be laid to rest and left undisturbed. On the Saturday night they heard the picks and shovels digging the graves they would shortly occupy.

At 8am precisely on the Monday the condemned men and their escort left the jail. The brothers were bare headed and without their usual neckerchiefs and wearing their normal moleskin clothes, though they had been freshly washed for the execution. The brothers were restrained by rope but able to make their way up the scaffold stairs unaided.

As the thousands stood in silence, the air was pierced with a screaming and the words "Oh, Mickey, Mickey, Mickey, my darling".

Michael, on hearing her, reportedly said to his brother, "Oh, there's Margaret!" It was reckoned the distraught woman was the lover of the older brother.

Having knelt and completed their prayers, the executioner, William Calcraft, stepped forward. He put on a close fitting black cloth cap, placed the noose of the rope round the neck of Peter, and tightened it over the cross beam. Having acted similarly to the older brother, he placed the white caps on top of their heads.

In their final words, both again pronounced their innocence and forgave their executioner. To the continuing shrieks from the woman in the crowd, the brothers kissed, Calcraft pulled their caps down, adjusted their position and, at 8.18am, withdrew the bolt.

The correspondents present at what was described as a "horrid and terrifying spectacle" believed the drop was little more than five inches and it took, according to some reports, up to five minutes for the young men's convulsive death-throes to end.

"One of the policemen nearly fell down the stairs of the scaffold," reported the Dundee, Perth & Cupar Advertiser, "and, on reaching the ground, swooned and had to be carried into an adjoining house where a medical gentleman attended him.

"The sky, which, till about ten minutes before was bright and gave promise of a scorching summer's day became suddenly overcast by black clouds, and heavy drops of rain began to fall which increased until it poured in torrents and quickly dispersed the crowd who ran in all directions for shelter.

"The drenching rain continued to fall till nine o' clock, at which hour the bodies were cut down and lowered into coffins beneath. They were shortly afterwards removed and interred within the precincts of the gaol."

By 10am the shops had reopened for business and by noon the scaffold had been disassembled and all traces of the grisly spectacle had been removed.

The Advertiser added: "A number of persons lingered in town till an advanced hour of the day, and among all the only subject of conversation was concerning the murder or execution and circumstances relating to them, and the numerous stories lost nothing by the frequency of relation; while superstitious old crones, with long drawn serious phrase, might here and there be heard pouring into eager ears favourite readings of the sudden change in the weather from bright sunshine to thunder-storm and shower during the time the unfortunate men were hanging, as auguring their innocence or guilt, or the happy or unhappy futurity of the deceased."

As the trusted voice of the town, the Fife Herald, whose staff would have been in the midst of events after the sentence, provides a more damning appraisal of the aftermath, and reached a conclusion that could be interpreted as either a cynical comment on human nature or a call for a penalty more shocking than the rope.

The newspaper stated: "Now came the time for the public houses, which were immediately filled to overflowing, and now commenced the scenes which disgraced our streets throughout the day. From this time nothing was heard but coarse and brutal jests, and the noise of Bacchanalian choruses resounding from the whisky shops.

"During the day, bands of men and women paraded the streets, some intoxicated, and almost all behaving most disgracefully. The terrible scene they had so lately witnessed was forgotten, or only remembered to furnish matter for a coarse jest or foul insinuation.

"Truly the terror of the law is a fiction if its most imposing phase is the scaffold and the hangman. If no more powerful motive to orderly conduct existed than the terror of the gibbet, judging from our streets on the day of the execution of the brothers Scanlan, we might bid adieu to public morality and decency for ever.

"But the gibbet is evidently not that terrible punishment, physically considered, which it is represented. There was none who saw the execution of Michael and Peter Scanlan, unless their experience was indeed very limited, but must have seen far more apparent suffering upon an ordinary deathbed.

"True it was a deprivation of life before its natural term was expired; yet the mere suffering, arising from the act of deprivation of life was not a punishment adequate to the crime – the punishment, if it must be equal to the offence, must be beyond a death by the hands of the executioner."

A race to secure mercy from the rope

While thousands clamoured in Cupar for a glimpse of the Scanlan brothers' execution, it would seem a generation later the public attitude to the death penalty was changing.

What was once a spectacle worth travelling many miles to witness was becoming a grotesque sentence where the finality of a judge's ruling was becoming increasingly perceived, at least in some quarters, as just as cold and callous as the actions that precipitated it.

That was particularly evident in the case of Edward Johnston.

Here was a case that, in 1908, had everything a gawping reader could possibly want. There was carnal indiscretion, infidelity, drunkenness, jealousy, violence, all wrapped up in poverty and desperation, and culminating in a brutal and bloody murder.

Johnston, Irish by birth and described as "reddish fair, and short in stature", was a coal mine brusher and had ended up in Steelend, a short distance from Saline, looking for work.

He and his partner, 24-year-old Janet Wallace Withers or Egleston, originally from Glasgow, had taken lodgings in the village. On the morning of Sunday, June 7, 1908, without any warning or disturbance, Johnston slit his lover's throat with an open razor, then took off towards Saline Hill. He was pursued, caught, handed over to the police and retained in custody at Dunfermline.

News of the killing quickly spread through the west Fife communities but the details of the couple's life leading up to the murder would command a wider audience.

That was helped by the prompt gathering of more colourful details for the national papers on the Monday morning, with an insight being given into what the Dundee Evening Telegraph described as the "sordid condition of affairs" that existed between the couple.

It was believed the victim was a married woman but estranged from her lawful husband, setting up home for a while in Kincardine with her new partner.

"Although depraved in their method of living, Johnston and Withers appeared to have had some sort of affection for each other," stated the Telegraph.

That may well have been the case but the relationship also seems to have been tempestuous with Johnston manifesting all the signs of coercive control, and that had culminated in violence in the past with him committing such serious assaults on his partner that he was jailed in July and December the previous year.

On his release the couple were reconciled but the clock was ticking down on Janet's life.

When Johnston was brought to trial in July, more flesh was put on the bones of the skeleton of the couple's lifestyle, and it was lurid stuff.

Appearing in a blue serge suit, Johnston, reckoned to be around 30 years of age, was calm and emotionless, with his defence entering a plea of not guilty because of insanity at the time of the killing, this "mental weakness" absolving him of responsibility for his actions.

Proceedings saw the heart-rending testimony of the victim's mother, Elizabeth, who tearfully told the court how her daughter had been beyond parental control from her mid-teens. She had seen the bruises inflicted upon her daughter by Johnston, with Janet admitting there were occasions when she was afraid of him, but also stressing his kindness when sober.

From the witnesses called, events leading up to the murder appear to have started on the Saturday.

Residents had enjoyed some revelry in Saline before returning to the lodging house that evening. All, at least on the surface had appeared well. Johnston, as he did in his usual attentiveness, unfastened and removed Janet's boots and filled his pipe for her to have a smoke.

How the evening progressed from there is unclear but the couple ended up sleeping in the kitchen while others retired. The next morning, when Johnston had decided to go to bed, Janet and her landlady entered the room, with the former nudging Johnston and, motioning to her companion, drew her finger across her throat.

A short while later, Johnston surfaced, entered the kitchen where he put his arm around Janet's neck and, seconds later, she dropped to the floor with blood pouring from her throat and neck. He then fled the house.

"Her head was nearly cut off," the landlady told the court.

"She tried to raise her head but failed, and the unfortunate woman gave one gurgle and never spoke a word," said her husband.

At that point a razor was produced as evidence and was confirmed as belonging to another of the lodgers. Called as a witness, he confirmed it was his.

In his statement Johnston had claimed this man had kissed Janet; she had recounted this and that was what prompted him to kill her. The witness denied any inappropriate involvement with Janet but Johnston, once apprehended, had cited this kiss as the trigger for his actions, stating that if his alleged wrongdoer had any manly decency he would "hang himself from the tallest tree in the wood".

After the description of the slaying, and the events leading up to it, the prosecution concluded in detailing the chase for Johnston who had fled into the countryside bareheaded, barefooted and wearing nothing but his trousers.

Medical evidence discounted Johnston's defence of temporary insanity and observation after his apprehension indicated a sound and clear state of mind. With that claim looking precarious, the defence case seems to have rested on mitigation, that being Johnston's perception of being cuckolded, and character testimony. The pair were generally seen as a loving couple, though violent exchanges had been observed, with blows mutually exchanged. Johnston himself was viewed as a quiet, hard working man and was well regarded by his employers.

With the case at its conclusion, the advocate-deputy told the court his duty was a painful one but that he thought this was a case where he was justified in asking for the full penalty of the law.

"The jury returned after an absence of fifteen minutes and unanimously found Johnston guilty of murder and strongly recommended him to the mercy of the court," reported the Dundee Evening Telegraph.

"Lord Ardwall, donning the black cap and addressing the accused, said the recommendation would be forwarded by him to the proper quarter. In the meantime his Lordship had no option except to pronounce the sentence that must follow a verdict of murder.

"His Lordship ordered that Edward Johnston be carried from the bar of Perth Sheriff Court to the prison of Perth, and, on 19th August, between the hours of eight and 10am be hanged by the neck until he was dead, and that by the hands of the common executioner."

According to the news reports the judge's closing remarks to Johnston were drowned out by the sobbing of the condemned man's relatives, a scene that greatly affected those in the courtroom.

"Johnston himself remained stolidly indifferent", reported the Telegraph, "although he tried to catch a passing glimpse of one of his relatives as he was being led downstairs."

"Indifferent" Johnston may have been, and so it would seem he remained. His violence towards and control over Janet Withers was brutal and unforgivable but it would seem the tragedy of this was weakness and a chaotic lifestyle. Johnston appears to have accepted justice was served and while the public accepted his guilt, it was less sure the rope was the appropriate punishment.

With little more than a month between trial and sentence, those keen to see the death penalty commuted had to move quickly. A fortnight before the execution date a petition was sent to the Scottish Secretary appealing for a reprieve. The grounds were the unanimous recommendation of the jury for mercy, evidence of Johnston's affection for the woman when not under the influence of drink, and the impulsive nature of the fatal assault.

The Dundee Courier highlighted the efforts, particularly those of Dunfermline solicitor George Crichton, to obtain the signatures of the jurors for the petition.

"Mr Crichton one day last week cycled to Kirkcaldy, thence to Largo and on to St Andrews," the newspaper reported. "He was successful in obtaining the signatures of fourteen of the fifteen jurymen. Altogether 639 signatures (not including those of the jury) were obtained in Dunfermline and Falkirk districts, made up as follows: Dunfermline burgh, 260; Falkirk, 208; Steelend, 157; and jurymen, 14. Johnston hails from Castlerdawson, Londonderry County, where a petition was signed by no fewer than 1590 names."

The week before the scheduled execution, according to the Montrose, Arbroath & Brechin Review of August 14, 1908, excitement was running high in Perth at the prospect of an execution, and the public was watching closely the efforts being made for a reprieve.

"The crime was a very sordid one, and public sympathy, though in some degree extended to the wretched man, is not altogether in favour of a remittal of the sentence," stated the Review.

"The prisoner himself is anxiously awaiting the result of the efforts which are being made by his solicitor and others on his behalf. He is kept daily informed and he is eagerly looking forward to the receipt of a message from the Scottish Secretary..."

"No communication has yet been received by the Magistrates of Perth that there is any possibility of a reprieve being granted, and arrangements have been made for the carrying out of the sentence. A scaffold is being sent on loan from Glasgow, and it is to be erected almost immediately in the prison yard.

"Pierpont, the executioner, has received instructions to hold himself in readiness to carry out the sentence..."

While Johnston waited for news he was kept in a special cell and guarded day and night.

The Review added: "He is allowed special privileges in the way of diet and literature, which are granted to those awaiting capital punishment, and though he fully realises the terrible position in which he is placed he is singularly cheerful.

"He appears to be grateful for anything which is done to make him more comfortable, and he conforms willingly to the prison rules.

"He is, of course, provided with a Bible and spends a good deal of time in reading it."

Hope, ultimately, proved futile as the authorities denied the plea for a commutation of sentence and, at 8am on Wednesday, August 19, 1908, Edward Johnston, widely described in the newspapers as the "Saline murderer" was led to the scaffold in Perth Prison to meet his maker.

Unlike the Cupar execution, the sentence was a 'closed' one and performed in front of a few officials and a handful of press representatives.

The Aberdeen People's Journal offered the public a sharp insight into the condemned man's last hours.

"The chaplain told me afterwards," said the Journal's reporter, "how wonderfully Johnston had shown his better nature and all who have come in contact with him speak of him as a man of a particularly gentle disposition."

"A brave chap" was how he was described after the execution with general agreement that given different circumstances he would have been a "sweet and reasonable human being".

Johnston was visited by the chaplain on the Tuesday evening, then went to bed, sleeping peacefully.

In the morning he was taken to a room near the scaffold, breakfasted and stayed with the chaplain until the end.

"You have prepared me well," Johnston reportedly told the chaplain, "and I wish Janet had had the same preparation before I hurled her into eternity."

As he prepared to be led to the gallows, Johnston declined to make any comment other than: "I have been treated with the utmost kindness since I came to the prison."

"The sad procession then moved from the room up the stair to the scaffold," the Journal report continued. "Bravely the hapless man stepped on to the trap door. An instant, and the straps were fixed, the rope arranged, the cap adjusted. and the lever drawn. In a silence made more profound by the whispered prayer of the chaplain the soul of the murderer fled. There were tears in the eyes of the strong men who saw Johnston die."

The doctor pronounced that death after the 7' 4" drop had been instantaneous. The prison bell rang out and a black flag hoisted to tell the silent crowd beyond the walls that the execution had been carried out.

Johnston's body was left to hang for an hour before being removed and buried in the prison yard beneath a simple stone stating "EJ – 1908", bringing an end to the tragic tale.

The poet who slowly faded from Fife's heritage

Fifers have made their marks in all walks of life. Science, the arts, sport, exploration, technology and innovation would all have shorter boundaries without that little bit of input from the ancient Kingdom.

And we like to celebrate those pioneers. Under the editorship of Allan Crow, the Fife Free Press for a number of years published an annual FP100. Contributions were sought from staff at all the company's titles with the East Fife Mail, Glenrothes Gazette, Fife Herald and St Andrews Citizen all putting forward suggestions for that year's topic, be it people, places or events.

Famous Fifers remains a popular subject either in a broad brush view or in specialist fields, and one that has proved a regular poll on Facebook's community pages, websites, as well as in the printed format.

The debate continues as to who was the 'greatest' of them all and, on occasions, even if he or she qualified as a Fifer at all.

In literature, the Kingdom's track record continues to flourish. While Val McDermid, Ian Rankin and the late Iain Banks may be the most familiar names to the general public, they are supported by the likes of Andrew Greig, Christopher Rush, Anne Smith, Joe Corrie, to name but a few. The lineage in poetry is a proud one as well, from the 19th century bairn 'Pet Marjorie' Fleming through to Eleanor Livingstone, artistic director with StAnza, Scotland's International Poetry Festival, held annually in St Andrews.

But the one thing they all have in common, whether their work is prose, poetry or song, is that Fife likes to think it cherishes them all.

But, actually, no, it doesn't.

While the depth of our home-grown talent increases, we perhaps need to trawl our archives to rediscover those Fifers who once shone brightly but have become the forgotten tellers of tales. Their loss from our heritage is sad, and unfair.

StAnza's reputation has flourished since it was founded in 1998 with a combination of productions and performances rightly winning it international acclaim. A few miles along the road from its St Andrews base is Kingsbarns and then Crail.

In 1904, a public lecture and concert was held in the East Neuk fishing burgh to commemorate one of the area's most famous sons. Yet today, if you look at the Crail Wikipedia page and the list of notable residents you won't find him listed alongside composer James Oswald (1710-1769), footballer William Dickson, (1866-1910), author Oswald Wynd (1913-1998) or Bletchley Park cryptanalyst Joan Clarke (1917-1996).

Our absentee writer was actually born in the smaller neighbouring village of Kingsbarns but here again he is absent from its list of fame that cites philosopher Robert Adamson (1852-1902), divinity professor and Church of Scotland Moderator Robert Arnot (1744-1808), New Zealand mine owner Alexander Peebles (1856-1934), musician James Yorkston (b. 1971), and presenter and journalist Vic Galloway (b. 1972).

Go into StAnza's website and type in his name and you'll draw a blank, and he's missing from all the comprehensive online lists of Scottish writers.

Given he was a well-published poet and popular songwriter, it remains bewildering as to why Fifers have forsaken and forgotten Thomas Carstairs Latto. In terms of impact in the early 19th century, Latto's works could be compared with those of Dunfermline's Robert Gilfillan (1798-1850) though history appears to have been slightly kinder to the west Fife poet and songwriter.

To be fair to all of us, and I definitely include myself, Latto doesn't seem to have been too concerned with self promotion and leaving a literary legacy. But, then again, his body of work should have ensured his place in Scottish literature and certainly in that roll call of famous Fifers. Crail Folk Club could well have one of his songs as the anthem for the end of each night's entertainment; StAnza could, perhaps, give a nod to the man who once bided just up the road and walked the streets the visiting poets now do every March.

My introduction to him only came when I stumbled upon that event in Crail Town Hall, held under the auspices of 'the Star of the East Lodge of Good Templars', and reported in the village columns of the East of Fife Record in November 1904.

From there, it was fairly easy to learn more, given you can find his work appearing in publications far and near, from the Blackwood and Tait magazines, to the Brechin Advertiser, the Newcastle Chronicle and the renowned Harper's Magazine in America.

But while he shone brighter and longer across the Atlantic, his fading place among the cast of Scotland's literary scene was well summarised in 1883 by D.H. Edwards in his Fifth Series of 'Modern Scottish Poets'.

From his Brechin office, Edwards wrote: "The author of some of the most widely-known of our Scottish lyrics is, perhaps, personally one of the most unfamiliar to the present generation of Scotsmen. His name was known and his songs were sung in Edinburgh when the Modern Athens was the favoured resort of choice and master spirits our age, when under the sheltering aegis of the great Christopher, Hogg and Aytoun, Moir and Riddle, Captain Gray, David Vedder, Alexander Smart and a hundred of the lesser lights of Scottish song gathered at the Old Fleshmarket Close and made the 'noctes' fly on golden wings. To Scotsmen of the present day, although his songs have lost none of their inspiring charm, the personality of the singer will scarcely be remembered."

How prophetic that was. So where does this long journey from celebration into obscurity begin?

Latto was born in 1818 in Kingsbarns, the eldest son of Alexander Latto, the village schoolmaster, and his wife, Christina Anderson.

According to Edwards' book, the young Thomas took positive traits from both his parents. From his father, a "deep moral sensibility" along with sharp intellect and natural empathy, while his mother's Norse blood fuelled a sense of independence.

He was just 14 when he was sent to St Andrews University, where he was the classmate of a number of distinguished scholars. He stayed in the Auld Grey Toun for five years where his poetic talents flourished and, according to Edwards, he was one of the few students given access to the university library.

In 1838 he moved to Edinburgh, taking up a position in the writing chambers of John Hunter WS. Three of his eight years in the capital were spent as Private Secretary to William Edmonston Aytoun, then Professor of Rhetoric at Edinburgh University. His singing and songwriting attracted attention but this also seems to have been a particularly creative spell in his writing, with him publishing 'The Minister's Kail Yaird', a volume of poems in Scottish dialect that received a positive response and is still available today.

He also made a number of contributions to the 'Whistle Binkie' anthology of songs. These collections were an emphatic nod to Robert Burns and while failing to impress the critics were widely appreciated by readers. Latto's works, which included 'The Kiss

Ahint the Door', 'When we were at the Schule', 'Sly Widow Skinner', and 'The Bonnie Blind Lassie' secured him a following.

But popularity and seemingly growing critical acclaim appears to have been an uncomfortable fit. He mixed with many of the leading literary lights but, apart from the occasional contribution, he shied away from publishing any more collections of his poetry.

From Edinburgh, he moved to Dundee as a managing clerk and then entered into business as a commission agent in Glasgow.

In 1851 he emigrated to the United States. This seemed to inspire a new lease of creativity and Latto was one of the founders and the first editor of the Scottish American Journal of New York. His writing was seen as key to the high regard in which the publication was held.

But he grew restless with that role and ended up in the newsroom of a Brooklyn daily paper, only occasionally returning to his creative writing.

In his later years, no doubt inspired by his mother's Viking heritage, he studied the Scandinavian languages and undertook translations of Danish, Norwegian, and Icelandic poetry.

In spring 1887, J.D. Ross, writing for the New York Home Journal, visited Latto at his family home in Bambridge Street, Brooklyn. It would probably be fair to say when you read the copy, Ross definitely combined his role of journalist with that of ardent fan.

He wrote: "The shades of evening were silently wrapping the snow-clad world in darkness as I entered the threshold of his comfortable home, and, with a feeling more of veneration than gladness, grasped the hand which he extended to welcome me.

"My visit shall live in my memory and be cherished as one of those rare events only met with at long intervals in the journey of life.

"It was the first time that I had stood in the presence of the author of many of the most familiar songs of my boyhood – songs which had charmed and delighted me with their extravagant humour and which now nestle among the happiest recollections of my early years. Nor was this the most important feature to me in connection with my visit to the talented songwriter and poet. Here was a man who had mingled with many of the illustrious men whose very names I had revered from infancy, and whose works had been a source of enjoyment and delight to me for so many long years – men who had made themselves famous by the treasures which they had added to, and by which they had enriched the general literature of Scotland, after which, laying aside their pen, they had passed from the world and joined one another in the 'Land of the Leal'."

After detailing his career and recounting literary acquaintances Latto had made in his life, Ross concluded: "He was noted among his schoolmates as being of a very reserved and retiring disposition, and, strange to say, these traits are characteristic of him even to this day.

"While his name and writing are well known throughout the United States and Canada, very few Scotsmen, even in this city are aware of the fact that their gifted countryman has resided for a number of years in a pleasantly-situated cottage in the suburbs of Brooklyn."

His death in March 1887 did make the news at home and his passing was widely covered by many journals in Scotland. He merited a well-shared tribute, an example of which can be found in the Ardrossan & Saltcoats Herald on Friday, November 20, 1896. It seems particularly apt to cite that publication as he shares his final resting column with an appreciation of his fellow Fifer, Robert Gilfillan.

Much of his work has been described, perhaps dismissed, as overly "sentimental" but isn't that the power of nostalgia, and a power that should be exercised to remember him?

An' are we but laddies yet,
An' get the name o' men?
How sweet at ane's fireside to live
Thae happy days again!
When we were at the schule, my frien',
When we were at the schule,
An' fling the snawba's owre again
We flang when at the schule.

'When we were at the Schule'
Thomas C. Latto

Embracing an illegal trade
in 'baccy' and brandy

There will be an obvious answer as to why most, if not all, Levenmouth councillors in the '60s and '70s referred to the area as the 'Barbary Coast'. As a young reporter this struck me as a label to underline the fierce, independent character of the communities; giving the adage 'it takes a lang spoon to sup' with a Fifer' some extra yardage.

But, of course, it might have had absolutely nothing to do with tribes of combative corsairs and, instead, referred to the red light district of mid-18th century San Francisco where wantonness and waywardness were the norm.

Both options do, however, share the traits of ignoring society's accepted rules and claiming a unique role in challenging authority.

And if there was one occupation that exemplified that more than any other, and employed many from St Andrews to Burntisland, it was that of the smuggler. Those involved in the 'trade' cut across all social strata, and with men, women and children all party to defying the government's revenue collectors.

Smuggling was a serious crime and, at one time, carried the death penalty but in a daily existence of hardship and austerity a black market in life's little luxuries, primarily 'baccy and booze', thrived.

Fife's prominence in the illicit trade has its place in history by providing the catalyst that sparked the Porteous Riots that broke out in Edinburgh in 1736. This followed the execution of smuggler Andrew Wilson who, along with two cohorts, carried out a daring robbery in Pittenweem while a customs collector slept. The story is recounted in some detail in Sir Walter Scott's 'The Heart of Midlothian' but Pittenweem, and the entire East Neuk, remained a smugglers' haven for many a year.

According to a historical feature in the Leven Advertiser & Wemyss Gazette in 1910, the entire Pittenweem community seems once to have been in cahoots when it came to smuggling.

In 1755 the 'Isabel and Mary' was seized by customs officials when it put into harbour laden with contraband. Four 'tide-waiters' were sent aboard to guard ship and cargo but during the night a crowd began to gather and, under the cover of darkness, a boarding party took over the vessel. The four customs men were locked up below deck and the contraband ferried ashore.

Audacious though that was, the mooring ropes were then cut and the 'Isabel and Mary' allowed to drift on to the rocks. The captives on board could well have perished if some benevolent locals hadn't rescued them. A reward of £50, the equivalent of around £11,000 in today's money, was put up for information that would lead to the capture of the perpetrators. It's not known if that was paid out but four men were apprehended and sent for trial though all walked free after the jury returned a not proven verdict. It would seem the destination of the contraband remained undetermined or unreported.

It is now generally accepted that the local powers-that-be tended to be somewhat sympathetic toward smugglers, probably to ensure their own decanters remained topped up from the trade. While the Pittenweem tale of the 'Isabel and Mary' was a grand scale effort, a few miles up the road in St Andrews, dodging the revenue men was a more open and regular practice.

An incident was recounted in the unattributed extracts of 'Smuggling Stories of Fife and Forfar' that was published in the Dundee Courier in 1911. The university town had a reputation for meeting the demand of locals and neighbours for 'duty free' goods and this occasion highlights the bravado exercised in dodging the government men.

The local customs controller spotted a group rolling two barrels of wine along the main road. Using the powers vested in him, he seized one of the hogsheads but the group made off with the other.

Determined to confiscate that cask and apprehend the culprits, he had a sentry stand guard over the seized barrel while he and his other officers made their way to a nearby inn where they suspected the illicit wine had been stashed. The landlord protested his innocence, but a maid guided the officers into an enclosed courtyard ... and then promptly locked them in.

Meanwhile a cry for help was heard from the street and the controller rushed to investigate, only to find his sentry felled on the ground and the hogshead disappearing around a corner.

With the officers duly freed from the courtyard, a search through the streets failed to produce any concealed barrels. The officials returned to the inn and, despite investigation, no contraband was found, and, ultimately, no arrests were made.

In both these north Fife cases, the central characters were local and the romantic notion is that the smuggler was a kent face in the community and, depending on the contraband, was either an independent 'trader', or a member of an organised group of such entrepreneurs. On occasions, such as the Pittenweem incident, we would end up with a 'Whisky Galore' scenario where an entire community was seemingly operating in collusion.

But the truth is a great deal of the illicit trade was directly between the Fife consumer and the European supplier. While Britain had a fairly tense relationship with France right up until the end of the Napoleonic wars, following that the Gallic entrepreneurs were welcomed with open arms, along with empty pipes and empty glasses.

In spring 1876, Dysart and the Wemyss area were the places to go if you needed tobacco or spirits. Such was the abundance of both that it naturally aroused suspicion with West Wemyss emerging as a primary source.

Coastguards were assigned to keep a close lookout on the area where, it was reported, a number of Frenchmen had been spotted; it was assumed they were up to no good, at least as far as customs revenue was concerned.

And it was two overweight gentlemen that caught the attention of one of the customs officers. They were stopped on the site of the new 'Dubbie' pit at Dysart, and, somewhat bizarrely, seemingly challenged over their rotundity.

It's hard to imagine what form the conversation took, but one of the Frenchmen insisted that their corpulence was real and naturally nurtured.

"Finding that the officer was bent upon searching them, one bolted amongst the machinery and furnaces of the new pit, and the other took down the braes in capital style, followed closely by the officer," reported the Dysart correspondent for the Dundee Courier in April 1876.

"Several complete somersaults among the bramble bushes took place, and the officer, like an experienced hound, again and again turned his game, until poor Frenchie bolted right into the tide, up to the neck, followed closely by the officer.

"When apprehended with an open knife in his hand, his bulky corporation turned out to be a number of now empty bladders, which, no doubt, had been full when the chase began.

"The employees at the pit had a real good jollification in the evening off the good things that had been 'planked' by Frenchie No.2."

Later that week a French vessel was boarded off West Wemyss with tobacco and gin being seized and the captain taken off his craft and escorted to Kirkcaldy, but still the flow of contraband continued. It was reported that brandy was arriving concealed in hampers covered with vegetables and crockery and tobacco hidden in oil and tar cans with false bottoms.

The correspondent's conclusion to his report, and the decision by the Courier to carry it, perhaps underlines the public attitude to the continental contraband: "Our shebeeners, 16 in all in Dysart, are laying in supplies, and Frenchie was never in better spirits than he appears to be in our streets," it read.

"Really their corporations exceed in girth those of the Kirkcaldy bailies; and under each arm one can see a small bundle about the size of a quarter loaf wrapped neatly up in a Glasgow block printed handkerchief, which contains about half a gallon of the famous 'Wemyss Brandy'.

"Should any of your Dundee readers feel curious for a sample, or, say, your police commissioners, your Dysart correspondent could with great facility oblige them."

By October that year, reports on the smuggling trade were almost becoming price comparison updates. Kippered salmon and sardines were selling a treat, primarily because they were actually concealing cake tobacco.

The cases had a wooden base, each holding 1lb of tobacco. Cigars, meanwhile, were arriving in jars labelled 'Preserved mutton' and were selling particularly well in Buckhaven and Methil. These would cost you a shilling {5p} for 20, while "best cake tobacco" was one and fourpence per lb, and inferior twist a shilling. The availability of brandy was also updated.

The newspapers also reported that owing to the bustle of the smugglers right along the north bank of the Forth, and the ongoing official efforts to curb the trade, the contraband was being insured with the payouts covering the fines the smugglers could expect in the Scottish courts.

The search for spies
and secret agents

While the government was far from chuffed at those corpulent 'Frenchies' wandering the coastline laden with illicit tobacco and brandy, come the turn of the century it was the suspected infiltration of the Germans that caused most concern as smuggling became secondary to spying.

Twenty years before the Great War, the 'mood map' of Europe was a tangled web of alliances with Britain, France, Germany, Russia, the Ottoman and Austro-Hungarian Empires all jostling for position in a new world order, with Japan and America fast-growing their imperialist ambitions.

It was a time of empires, be they growing or crumbling, and Britain, from its position of 'splendid isolation' was keen to ensure that the sun would continue to never set on its sphere of influence, and Fife had a role to play in that.

History, on its most simplistic level, illustrates a Europe that was preparing for war – nobody wanted one but it was better to be prepared.

Britain's relationship with Germany had been cordial, even friendly. Prime Minister Lord Salisbury and Chancellor Bismarck maintained a balance and a formal alliance between the two nations was considered, though never followed through. However, the ousting of Bismarck by Kaiser Wilhelm II changed all that. The Kaiser was keen to see Germany gain strength, and influence, and become a major naval power.

Britannia, of course, ruled the waves and wasn't keen to see any challengers to her maritime dominance. The Royal Navy was muscled up and Rosyth was key to that, giving Fife a major strategic role in Britain's global perspective and goals. In 1903 the government approved a £3m package, excluding machinery, to develop the dockyard. In today's money that's in excess of £360m, so it was a major national investment in the country's security.

In January 1909, Major A.J. Reed, secretary for the Perthshire branch of the Primrose League, an organisation committed to spreading the Conservative message, made the headlines by seemingly confirming German spies had been active in the Rosyth area.

Speaking at a Unionist meeting in Blackford, Reed claimed that Britain's intelligence services had confirmed there was an estimated 1500 German secret agents operating in Scotland, and 5000 nationally.

They were split into two sections. First there were the fixed agents, dubbed 'letter boxes' in the spying fraternity. These came from various nationalities and were in all walks of life. Their mission was to compile reports on the coastal defences, utilities, railways, supply chains, etc.

The second section was "travelling agents", such as commercial travellers, and they organised espionage and ran the network of fixed agents.

Reed asserted that, over the past two years, the whole of Scotland's defences had been secretly investigated and reported back to Berlin.

The Major's comments received a national platform and, although still five years away from the assassination in Sarajevo of Archduke Franz Ferdinand of Austria which would begin the chain of events leading to the outbreak of war, Germany was already the villain, and Fife became increasingly suspicious of any foreign visitors.

The importance of the Rosyth dockyard was highlighted by the Dundee Courier in August 1912 when it stated: "When completed, the dockyard will constitute the principal defences in the northern shores of the country.

"It is well known that when the Unionist Government first secured the ground on the northern shore of the Forth and decided to establish there a first class naval base, they were looking to possible attack from the Germans across the North Sea.

"It can also be assumed that with a secret service which equals, if not outrivals, that of all other nations, the Germans have made certain that they will be furnished with information regarding the extent, situation, and surroundings of the new dockyard."

That introduction preceded a strange case involving two foreign gentlemen, one reckoned to be in his 20s and the other around ten years older, who had checked into the Queen's Hotel in Inverkeithing.

The pair declared themselves missionaries, but the locals were having none of that with everyone apparently convinced they were spying on the nearby dockyard for the Fatherland.

It was reported that the two men kept to themselves and rarely spoke to others. While such behaviour would appear to actually arouse suspicion, their routine also made them stick out like sore thumbs.

After breakfast, the men took to wandering the area; fuelling speculation they were scouring for vantage points to study the dockyard. It was noted, however, these excursions were always taken without a camera.

This espionage threat was taken so seriously that Britain put its own disguised agents on the case to closely tail the suspects.

The Dundee Courier reported that there was no doubt the pair were German, a magistrate assuring this because of the way they carried their knapsacks, wore their cloaks and their "general bearing".

It was established the suspected spies had not attempted to breach the security surrounding the dockyard, though it was confirmed it was possible they had been able to get very close to the work going on at Rosyth by buying a ticket for one of the pleasure steamers from Aberdeen or Bo'ness which offered clear views of the dockyard from its decks.

After three days, the 'spies' took the ferry across the Forth and dropped out of sight.

"During their stay in Inverkeithing the strange pair made no effort to hide the fact they were not Britishers," reported the Courier.

This incident, as reported at the time, has enough flaws in it for it to be interpreted as more farcical than sinister. The two men's apparent determination to stand out from the crowd in accent, appearance and actions, certainly implies they were bottom of the class at spy school.

But while this might be dismissed as local paranoia created by ongoing propaganda, after the outbreak of war the Rosyth dockyard and the Fife coastal defences were undoubtedly of prime interest to Germany.

The mood of "spies here, there and everywhere" was further heightened at the start of the conflict with the publication of the book 'The Secrets of the German War Office' by Dr Armgaard Karl Graves.

This self-confessed secret agent had claimed spying was rife around Rosyth and that a German infiltrator had been arrested who was for some time in charge of the telephone department in the dockyard.

His role had allowed him to eavesdrop on the conversations concerning all stages of the construction work.

In November 1914, the Earl of Crawford and Balcarres raised the temperature even higher when, addressing the House of Lords, he said Fife continued to be in a "most unsatisfactory condition" as regards the alien danger.

The Earl, whose country estate sat above Colinsburgh, pointed out that, despite recently imposed rules, "alien enemies" continued to live in Fife, coming and going at their "own sweet wills".

Reporting the Earl's speech, the St Andrews Citizen stated: "Up to last week there was actually an alien enemy living in the county to whom the Home Office had refused naturalisation. That alien resided at a spot commanding the sea. Next door but one to him was another, who made no secret of his well-wishing to the German Army. He habitually and contemptuously expressed his views about ours. At the extreme east end of Fife had resided, til the end of August, a German who was detected tampering with official messages sent along the coast to the coastguard. That person was removed, but somehow he persuaded the authorities that he was innocent, and he came back to Fife and the only penalty he incurred was that he was cut off from the telephone. On 29th October he was removed, but he {Lord Crawford} was not certain he would not get back again."

The House of Lords was told that night signalling from the Fife shoreline was continuous and Lord Crawford claimed he could give the names of six places within a few miles of Colinsburgh where this had been going on.

"One of these persons was discovered to have filled up a form of questions submitted to him from Germany" stated the Citizen. "Another form of communication with the enemy, which had been discovered recently, was a very carefully prepared system by post so arranged as to escape the activities of the Censor."

Lord Crawford went on to claim the Forth was full of German sailors, crewing neutral ships. He believed small quantities of dynamite were being smuggled and even secret mine laying operations taking place.

In conclusion he believed the authorities should be granted the power to remove any naturalised British subject of German birth who was open to reasonable suspicion. The situation was deemed dangerous with many German subjects still residing in prohibited areas. He also cited cases where husbands had been moved but the wives and sons had been allowed to remain.

Any crackdown on Germans wasn't an easy task. Given the earlier warm relations between the two countries, Britain had welcomed over 100,000 German immigrants, and all, including their families, were now seemingly worth scrutiny. Nationally control was being tightened; there was even debate over the possibility of mass deportations.

But Lord Crawford's focus on the situation in Fife brought a quick response from Thomas McKinnon Wood, Secretary for Scotland, which was widely reported, including in the columns of the Wigan Observer & District Advertiser.

Addressing the issue of the number of Germans in Fife, he was reported as stating: "With the exception of five or six at Kirkcaldy, there were no male alien enemies above sixteen years of age in the whole county of Fife at the time when your speech was made.

"You refer to the case of a German spy who you say was detected tampering with official messages. It is true that he was arrested ... and that he was discharged, for the reason that no evidence was found against him.

"It is not, therefore, correct to say that he was detected tampering with official messages."

The Scottish Secretary went on to say night signalling was seen as a very serious matter but no single act had been proved and while he would not contradict Lord Crawford's claims he gave his assurance that no effort would be spared to investigate suspicious cases and to "institute such preventive measures as shall make night signalling a very difficult and dangerous operation".

But concern persisted. Towards the end of the year it was reported that the military authorities were receiving numerous sightings of possible spies, along with reports of mysterious lights and movements.

"The latest developments come from Kinghorn and Kirkcaldy," reported the Dundee Evening Telegraph on November 19, 1914.

"At the former place a house situated near the end of the beach, and which has a good view of the Kinghorn fort, is being closely watched by the authorities, and although nothing incriminating has actually been seen, our Kirkcaldy representative learns that the authorities have good reason to believe that messages are being received and despatched from this neighbourhood."

It was reported a foreign couple who holidayed in the area were being investigated and "uneasiness" prevailed in Kirkcaldy after a six-foot tall individual of foreign and military appearance had been observed "wandering about", even as far inland as Auchtertool. Members of the public were asked to be on their guard and advised to contact the authorities if they saw this Homburg-wearing, light-yellow booted, clean-shaven suspect.

Given Reed's legion of 'letter boxes', Inverkeithing's 'missionaries impossible', Lord Crawford's string of sinister signallers, and Kirkcaldy's secretive stranger, it would be tempting to mock those overt operatives as a manifestation of a form of mass wartime hysteria. Indeed, it seems officially most of these reports, if not all, were without any real substance. Nevertheless, Fife, and especially Rosyth, had strategic significance and any covert operations carried out by the Germans could add more lives to the rising death toll, and spies were not a figment of the imagination.

Rosyth was high on the list of targets of at least three agents, as their trials would reveal.

History has recorded the names of the German spies uncovered by British Intelligence and a Fife link to some prominent names – Carl Hans Lody, George Traugott Breeckow (aka Reginald Rowland) and Louise 'Lizzie' Wertheim. All spied on Rosyth and that contributed to their fate.

Lody was the first spy to be executed in the Tower of London during the war, facing the firing squad on Friday, November 6, 1914. Operating under the alias of Charles A. Inglis he was tasked in the opening months of the war to spy on the naval traffic in the Firth of Forth. Though based in Edinburgh, he hired a bicycle and visited Rosyth to gather information.

Although apparently cool and collected, and accepted as a tourist, he lacked spying sophistication.

"Lody was detected in his very first message home, which had been sent to an Adolf Buchard in Stockholm. MI5 knew that this address was a cover for German intelligence. Any messages sent there were intercepted and Lody's correspondence made it clear that a German spy was active in Britain," states the MI5 report.

He only operated in Scotland for a month before being apprehended and was the only spy to go on public trial. He was undoubtedly a patriot and his demeanour did win him some sympathy but calls to commute his death sentence failed as his execution was seen as providing a deterrent.

But Rosyth was very much a prime target for Breeckow and Wertheim.

He arrived in England in May 1915 on a fake American passport. Having spent much time in the States he, like Lody, easily fitted into the role of tourist and adopted the name Reginald Rowland. His contact in London was Wertheim, a woman of Polish-German origins with a shady and colourful background.

The two became recognisable figures in the capital's cosmopolitan scene with Wertheim making the most of Breeckow's expense account from his paymasters, so much so he actually complained about her extravagance.

Their differences led to the spying duties being divided with Wertheim charged with soliciting the information and Breeckow passing it on. So, in the company of a maid, she travelled between London and Rosyth to gather what information she could on the Grand Fleet.

She stayed in the best hotels when in Scotland and as attractive, well-dressed and immediately accepted by all as a British woman, she was successful in her mission. However, her questioning did arouse suspicion. Meanwhile Breeckow's intercepted letters about his excursions with 'Lizzie' completed the jigsaw and both were arrested.

The two went on trial at the High Court in September 1915, just four months after their spying relationship had begun.

Breeckow was sentenced to death and was executed by firing squad at the Tower of London on October 26, 1915.

Wertheim, seen to be under the influence of her accomplice, received a 10-year jail sentence. In 1918, as her mental health deteriorated, she was transferred from Aylesbury Prison to what was then Broadmoor Criminal Lunatic Asylum where she died of pulmonary tuberculosis in July 1920.

The beet generation
of Lewis Adventurers

The Fife Adventurers and their ill-advised and ill-fated 'colonisation' of the Isle of Lewis in the dying years of the 16th century has a firm place in Scottish history, though shrouded in regal, cultural, economic and political shame.

Less well known are the 'Lewis Adventurers' who were a much more convivial band and their brief stay in Fife was warmly welcomed and remembered.

The Kingdom has opened its doors and its arms to many an incomer through the centuries.

Maybe best to leave the Romans to one side but there was the Auld Alliance with France, safe ports for Spanish Armada stragglers, the exiled Polish servicemen in World War Two and then, a few years later, the Long Islanders arrived.

And their departure from the Outer Hebrides in the early 1950s was such sweet sorrow ... literally because what brought them to the ancient Kingdom on Scotland's east coast was sugar.

Their destination was the county town of Cupar, the location of Scotland's only beet plant.

Built in 1926 by the Anglo-Scottish Beet Sugar Corporation and taken over in 1936 by the British Sugar Corporation, the factory had fluctuating fortunes in establishing a viable place of production in a soaring market.

As a seasonal industry, the Cupar factory had to cast its net wider and wider to find the labour it needed, transporting workers by bus from Levenmouth and Kirkcaldy in the industrial heartland of Fife.

In March 1951, with plans to radically modernise the processes and a new target imposed of a throughput of 2000 tons of beet per 24 hours, manpower became a crucial issue and, with seasonal labour in short supply, the bosses looked north.

Lewismen and women were no strangers to travelling to where there was work during the quieter periods of the crofting and fishing calendar, so, after discussions with the Ministry of Labour, it was decided to build hostels on the factory site for 100 men.

The Dundee Courier in early September 1951 revealed that the general manager of the Cupar plant had visited Lewis and preliminary arrangements had already been made on importing workers.

"A representative of the factory will travel to Stornoway soon to make final arrangements," the Courier reported.

"Two young Lewis men are already at the factory helping to build the hostels. Despite difficulties in obtaining supplies the work is now progressing rapidly, and it is expected they will be ready early in October."

And a few weeks later, the Fife Herald, which was based in Cupar, announced the arrival of the Lewis men in colourful style.

"They have come – the Macleods, the Macivers, the Mackenzies and the Morrisons – to the Kingdom of Fife, in fact to our very doorstep," proclaimed the Herald.

"They are the flaxen-haired men of the Western Isle of Lewis, the land of fairies and whisky galore.

"Are they the descendants of those miscreants who, 400 years ago, cut off the heads of the Fifers who exploited the fishing of Lewis and sent back their heads pickled in barrels?"

Despite that rather garish opening turn of phrase, the Herald's report on Wednesday, October 24, 1951, quickly assured Cuparians that the visitors' minds were not on slaughter but sugar and welcomed the town's new arrivals into the community.

The deadline to build the hostels had been met, but only just, with just a few days to spare before the new workers took up residence.

But, thanks to the weather, not everything had gone smoothly since.

The manager of the local bus depot, Mr J. Heggie, had left Fife with three buses on a Tuesday morning to transport the Lewismen to Cupar.

He and the drivers put up at a hotel at Kyle of Lochalsh, arranging a 4.30 call on Wednesday morning so they could meet and greet the boat from Stornoway, which was due to dock at 5.30am.

But the boat failed to arrive and, probably given the time of the day, there was no answer to the calls put into the Stornoway shipping office.

The Fifers were obviously unaware of the unpredictability of the Minch as they learned later that a storm had delayed the sailing.

It eventually arrived, and the buses made their way via Invergarry to Dalwhinnie where it had been arranged for the men to have breakfast.

Unfortunately, because of the delay, the convoy reached the hotel just when the guests were finishing lunch.

However, staff managed to cobble together some form of brunch and by 3pm the party was back on the road and heading towards Cupar.

That wasn't straightforward either with the buses struggling on some of the narrow roads and, on a couple of occasions, even having to reverse to deal with hairpin bends.

The journey finally ended at around 7.30pm when the weary workers reached their hostels.

"Before the bus journey, there had been the stormy crossing of the Minch," reported the Fife Herald, "but the least said about that the better, for the Lewismen admitted it was the worst crossing they had experienced.

"When they arrived at the factory they had a meal and went straight to bed in the hostel built for them.

"The following morning they were kept busy with form-filling, medical inspection, and being shown what jobs they would do."

In that first party to arrive in Fife there were 93 men – 29 were Macleods, and 17 of these were Murdos!

Their ages ranged from 19 to 44 and all had been on the mainland before, some of them completing their National Service.

Several of the men had left wives back in Lewis.

One of the single men was 22-year-old Donald J. Maciver who was interviewed by the Fife Herald.

"Donald, who did his National Service with the Seaforths and a spell of training at Stobs camp this year, said he thought he and his colleagues were going to enjoy the work very much," reported the Herald.

"Back home they worked on the crofts during the summer and wove Harris tweed in their homes during the winter. Most of them also did a bit of fishing for they owned their boats.

"The weaving industry, however, was not paying due to the demand having fallen. They were going to earn more at the beet sugar factory than they could make at home.

"Asked about the weather, Donald said he found it much the same here as at home.

"He was enjoying the food and he and his pals were delighted with the accommodation afforded them.

"The men will not lack entertainment during the winter nights – they go home in late December – for they intend to hold several ccilidhs. When by themselves they talk in Gaelic, and that has its advantages when they are working in the factory – their displeasure can always be voiced in a freer manner!

71

"The Macleods have challenged the other clans to a football match, and this looks as if it will be one of the highlights of their stay."

The similarity in names was obviously a problem, especially among the Murdo Macleods.

So, to get over the difficulty for the local postman of the 17 'Murdos', each man's mail would, in addition to his name and address, have upon it his works number – army fashion.

Had it not been for the numbers the men had been allotted, the factory official who travelled with them from Lewis would not have known to which member of the party he was talking on the trip across.

Probably, because of National Service, the hostel accommodation wouldn't have been too strange a set-up. It consisted of three different dormitories, one for each shift of 30 men.

This enabled one shift to come off duty and another to go on without waking the third.

The working hours saw the dayshift on from 8am to 4pm, the backshift from 4pm to midnight, with the nightshift running from midnight through to 8am.

"The dormitories have all the fittings of home, and the men are really comfortable," said the Herald.

"There is a small shop where the men can buy requirements, such as soap, razor blades, toothpaste, towels etc.

"A question which may be asked is: Will they come back?"

According to reports, some of the men were hardly in the factory when they were volunteering for the refining run next summer, and, according to Donald Maciver, they would be back the next winter if required.

The Herald continued: "The management of the factory think highly of the men.

"The islanders are of a high standard of intelligence, and they are bound to prove more than generally useful during the hectic beet campaign.

"The men wish to be home in time for Hogmanay but till then they hope to enjoy the work and pleasures here.

"During the war many of them served with the Royal and Merchant Navy, yet they are of a shy disposition.

"Yes, those Macleods, Macivers, Mackenzies, Morrisons, and the others, are going to take back to their kinsfolk tales of the hospitality of the people of East Fife and there should be established a link between Fife and Lewis which will never be broken.

"Here the men see the doorway to a prosperity denied them on their island home."

During their time at the factory, the Lewismen worked a 56-hour week, and would have had over £6 clear after paying for their board.

The first visit certainly did prove to be a success.

The company's house magazine that year carried a special feature on the Lewismen's stay, featuring pictures of the men at work and play, alongside an outline of clan history!

Hogmanay at home proved to be possible for the Lewis group with the final bag of sugar being filled at 10pm on Friday, December 28. There is no record as to whether the weather conditions were kinder for the return journey across the notorious Minch.

"The factory officials have been well satisfied with the men on the whole," stated the Fife Herald on Wednesday, January 2, 1952.

"It is believed that, with very few exceptions indeed, the men have been content and happy in their work, and there is no doubt that many firm friendships have been established and that these will be renewed and strengthened when the men come back again."

And so it was, in fact just a few weeks later, the factory decided to recruit 50 men on the cane sugar refining lines. They were wanted in mid-March for at least three months.

That autumn saw 100 jobs on offer in Fife and, this time, the applications in Lewis topped 170.

A.P. Winton, the welfare and labour officer at the factory, had been highly pleased with the calibre of the men the previous year and, when he visited Stornoway in September, over 200 had been called for interview by the Stornoway Employment Exchange.

That initial number was whittled down as some of those called were unable to leave home for domestic reasons, and a few refused to consider the offer of work at Cupar because the factory operated continuously seven days a week, thus violating the Sabbath.

With 170 names on his list, Mr Winston told the Stornoway Gazette: "I would take them all – if we had the hostel accommodation. They are all suitable."

The final selection was to be made when Mr Winton re-turned to Cupar. Everybody would be notified, whether he was accepted or rejected.

"Those who are rejected must not think we have anything against them. It is just that we can't take everybody," said Mr Winton.

Forty of those who were at Cupar the previous year were signed on again. Many of them wrote in again as soon as they heard jobs were available.

Some of the written applications were difficult to deal with because they had come from the mainland, there was the clash of names and they hadn't given their previous works number.

But one applicant was readily identified.

His letter read: "Dear Mr Winton, "Could I please have my old job back in the limehouse? I enjoyed myself and would like to get back with the boys in the limehouse again. Yours faithfully. Donald Macdonald (Feedoh). P.S.—Will I bring my bagpipes?"

Mr Winton replied: "Dear Feedoh Thank you very much for your letter. You certainly can start again at your old job. We were very pleased with your services. P.S.—Bring your bagpipes."

The selected 100 would sail from Stornoway on the Loch Seaforth in early October. No doubt those who had signed up for a second trip to Fife were hoping for a calmer crossing than their adventure in 1951.

A hero on hand
to save the day

Entertain, inform and educate – as said before these were always the supposed original three prime aims of newspapers. The arrival of broadcast media and, of course, more recently the digital age and social media, has seen those honourable aims expanded, and blurred.

Titillation, confusion, misinformation, sensationalism are now also in general use where every tactic is employed in the online clickbait war. A smutty headline on a non-story can attract thousands of 'visitors' who are undoubtedly less discerning about the validity or worth of the tale below it.

Yet, despite the technological advancements and the changes in our reading habits the genuinely 'good story' still wins out. These still pop up all over the place. The courtroom, though now visited much less frequently by reporters, was always a prime source for compulsive reading material.

A trawl through any newspaper's archive will produce court cases that astonish, horrify, bewilder or amuse but, then again, that is to be expected since the legal process is there to sanction human frailties.

Rarer are the bizarre tales that defy explanation, and some publications have devoted themselves to the inexplicable and, often, unverifiable.

But there is another category, one that produces stories that are a joy to write as well as to read; those extraordinary tales that involve ordinary folk. Whether it's a granny tackling a housebreaker or an airport worker challenging a terrorist, the scenario allows us to imagine what we would do in a similar situation, and allows us to celebrate those inspiring actions.

Among those incidents that make the headlines are rescues, where the man, woman, child and, on occasions, pet, leap from the humdrum to heroic. Unfortunately, these characters to the reader really only do have their metaphorical 15 minutes of fame but for those they rescued their names last a great deal longer, perhaps forever. Here are a few names Fifers should doff their caps to and, at least briefly, enjoy their stories, realising they are but a tiny section of a huge crowd united by courage and quick thinking.

Let's start with 13-year-old Joseph Yorke, a youngster who, in 1932, lived with his grandmother in Beveridge Place,

Lumphinnans. The lad went out one June evening to catch minnows at the golf course pond when he heard some girls screaming.

He ran to investigate to find a three-year-old sinking below the surface in front of the helpless onlookers.

Joseph didn't hesitate and plunged in to help the drowning toddler but there was a problem, the would-be rescuer couldn't swim either.

A man who was passing by offered Joseph his hand and the teenager clutched it, allowing him to stretch far enough to grab the child and haul him to the bank.

The toddler was unconscious so Joseph, the man and then a passing doctor, all tried to resuscitate him, their efforts finally paying off and the lad revived.

"I got a fright when I saw him disappearing below the water," Joseph told the Dundee Evening Telegraph.

" I never thought of the danger when I went into the water, as all I wanted was to save the wee laddie and I'm awfully glad that he wasn't drowned.

"I thought I had been too late as I saw him lying on the ground with his lips so blue. I don't know who the man was that helped me to get him out as he just went away."

When bravery was suggested on his part the teenager said: "I jist did what ony ither chap would have dune."

It was another non-swimmer being hailed the hero in July 1937, this time at the popular beauty spot of Aberdour sands.

Eight-year-old John Rafferty, from Clydebank, was playing on the beach and scrambled aboard a disabled motor boat. Unfortunately, the vessel was taken into tow and hauled into deeper water. John panicked and ended up overboard.

James Duff, from the Stirling area, spotted the lad in difficulty and without even shedding any clothes, and being unable to swim himself, plunged into the water. By the time he reached John, the boy had gone down twice but he managed to struggle back to shore holding the youngster's head above the water.

Several holidaymakers, who had witnessed the drama, immediately applied artificial resuscitation and the boy recovered. Although shaken, the youngster was none the worse after his terrifying ordeal.

The next hero in the headlines again wasn't a Fifer but his visit to the Kingdom proved to be a godsend, and he certainly didn't do what "any other chap would have done".

This story comes from the end of August 1948 and involves another potential drowning, this time off St Andrews.

Fourteen-year-old James Johnston from Methil was on a camping holiday with his parents and decided to spend some time playing on the beach.

Unknown to his parents, he managed to borrow a rubber dinghy and took to the water at the East Sands.

A wind was picking up and the lad was soon being swept out to sea. Fortunately for him, also enjoying a day on the beach was Robert Campbell, an instructor at Glasgow Eastern Swimming Club. He saw James frantically waving his arms and realising the boy was now in serious danger, Mr Campbell, left his wife and child on the beach, dived in and began his solo pursuit of the dinghy.

He eventually caught up with it around a mile offshore, but then came the problem of what to do next. He couldn't ask the lad to "abandon ship" and carry him a mile back to safety ... but there was a short tethering rope.

So Mr Campbell grabbed that with his teeth, turned back towards St Andrews and starting swimming.

Speaking later, after being helped and landed by local fishermen, the Leven Mail reported: "He opened his mouth, and showed two rows of strong teeth. 'Look, there's where I held the rope,' he said. 'It was worse after I left the shelter of the shore. The dinghy seemed to be going very fast'."

They said
they were Celtic

Not all aspects of Fife's past are chronicled in the local newspapers. Certainly, there are spin-off tales of accidents and court cases but daily life was routine and when it passed it did so gradually and without much notice.

One of those was the phenomenon of 'visitors', when the Glasgow area seemed to empty for the Fair Fortnight and thousands of families left the city to go "doon the watter"... or take up a brief seaside residence somewhere different, and the Fife coast was one of those destinations.

Two weeks in the Spanish sun was unimaginable then; there weren't glossy brochures and pre-booking, while an absolute necessity, involved a lot of legwork, and knocking.

You'd be sitting at the kitchen table having your soup and pudding on a winter's afternoon when there would be chapping on the door. On the step would be total strangers, with just one question: "Do you take visitors?"

First impressions would be important and if you did indeed take 'visitors' and you liked the look of them, there would be a brief discussion, terms agreed, arrival and departure dates set, and that would be it, deal done.

Come the Fair, would come the adventure. My sister and I, along with our parents relocated to the back bedroom, along with a Primus stove, and we would camp there for a fortnight, giving over the rest of the house to the visitors. They would have the run of the living room with 'folding bed', the 'good' room with the bed settee, the other bedroom and the scullery, with the toilet and bath the only shared facilities.

They would come and go as they please, returning from the pub or the Gunners' Club after closing time a little noisier than when they left, but it all seemed to work well enough.

I actually have no memories of any real contact with those visitors, no bonding or lasting friendships but we had neighbours who had the same folk return year after year and they became regular fixtures every summer as they whiled a few hours soaking up the sun in the shared back green.

Although we didn't become the best of friends, there were, on occasions, Christmas cards exchanged and everyone was friendly and polite during the stay.

There was one instance of tension I do recall though. The family we had staying had daughters in their teens. Not long before the summer, my father decided the bathroom needed a bit of a spruce-up so it was given a lick of paint and, despite the hereditary lack of any DIY skill, he laboriously fitted vinyl floor tiles.

The visitors hadn't been there a day when my father was horrified to discover what the teenagers' stilettos had done to his handiwork. The hundreds of little dimples as the girls pouted in front of the bathroom mirror were reminders of our visitors for many a year after.

While evening revelry was very much on the cards for those hundreds of visitors, and understandably so as a two-week respite from the humdrum of the daily grind and the city tenements, the Leven of the late 1950s and early '60s was very much a holiday town, and you could see its attractions, though much of those have faded or disappeared now.

But there are old postcards that pop up here and there that show just how packed the promenade used to be, and that really was the prime attraction for the visiting families during the day.

There was the West End Cafe, Doriano's ice cream hut, the Festival Gardens, the Beach Hotel, putting green, giant draughts, paddling pool, the swings, the Beach Pavilion and, of course, the sands stretching around Largo Bay.

Behind the seafront the town had pubs, clubs and cinemas and there was Letham Glen with entertainment at the bandstand adding to the walks and the gardens. There were also the golf courses though a bag of clubs never seemed to be among the luggage of our temporary lodgers.

If you had the weather, Leven did offer a comfortable break, and it was a glory that lingered in reputation long after the faded reality. During what is known in the media as "the silly season", one regular 'soft' feature was for the East Fife Mail in the late 1970s to send staff along the prom' to solicit comments from holidaymakers on how much they were enjoying their stay in the town.

By this time, the era of the visitors had long passed; Levenmouth's prosperity was on the wane. There was plenty of room between the putting green pins and the trampolines had lost a lot of their bounce. The intro' on the filed feature began: "Holiday resort or last resort ..." The editor viewed that as sullying the town's good name and his red pen went to work, but it was probably the last time that holiday season feature ran.

But those glory days had the town buzzing and it would start to creak at the weekend with the convoys that rolled in with day trippers.

The car park at the west end of Leven prom' is still there but now with a more enduring surface than the red blaes that accommodated so many buses from the Glasgow area over the summer period.

Aesthetically, some would argue the seafront of Leven was spoiled by the power station and its towering lum but that was the end you turned your back on as Largo Bay beckoned before you. It was perhaps a fitting 'bookend' to the prom'. Looking east, there was the beach, the 'sea', and the shoreline seemingly stretching all the way to Kincraig Point. Behind you stood industrial Methil, and a way of life that was probably a reminder of the routine. A brief soujourn to the seaside was nothing less than a tonic.

Across the road from this 'coach park' was the West End Cafe. Fronted by an ice cream and candy floss kiosk, within lay a dimly lit tea room where the waitresses all wore black with white pinnies, and had notebooks dangling. A few paces along the road and up Seagate was the Buckie House with such exotica as a parrot, budgies, canaries, a monkey, a fox ... all housed in shell-covered enclosures; there was even a buckie bus.

You were close enough to smell the fish and chips wafting over from the Shorehead. It wasn't a bad arrival but ahead of you were the golden 800 yards, the gentle waters of the Forth, the beach, ice cream – available from hut, van and kiosk – the gardens and a cold beer at the hotel.

But there was one other feature, stretches of grass from the edge of the bus park, all the way to the caravan site that bordered the links, all offering the space for that impromptu football match.

And it was on this turf an event occurred, important to Fife's sporting heritage. I was there and it is possibly true. I say possibly as, over half a century later, details don't just become blurry they become redefined. A possible becomes a definite and some definites were never possible.

But it is worth repeating here because it could easily have happened. If it didn't, it should have, and something very similar could have, and probably did.

So where do we begin? Well, remember when Scotland won the World Cup in April 1967?

I know the tournament was in 1966 but then we beat the champions, though for the life of me I can't remember their name so, fair's fair, the title was ours. Then, after claiming the World Cup, it seemed only fitting the European Cup was next. So, on May 25, 1967, Celtic did just that with a 2-1 victory over Inter Milan at the Estadio Nacional near Lisbon.

And so it came to pass that near the end of the summer in 1967, Leven Prom set the scene for a local sporting occasion which, until this day, has never been officially recognised.

The venue for this great spectacle was that stretch of grass between where Doriano's green wooden cafe once stood and the bus park. The path that leads to the steps down to the beach was at the back of one set of 'goals', the other set was down near where the grass ran out to meet the car park.

On one side was a group of local lads and on the other, well, they were blokes off one of the buses.

All summer we used to wait and watch them roll in and roll off, winklepickers, Brylcreem, sharp suits, accompanied by wives and girlfriends in high-heels and short skirts.

The Glasgow boys, after a few refreshing glugs of Export, would treat their women to a Sweetheart Stout and an ice cream, then off would come the jackets, in piles a few paces apart, out would come the football and, suddenly, it was Hampden.

That was our cue.

"Fancy a game," one of us would shout.

"Aye, a'right then", a Brylcreem-slicked winklepicker-wearer would usually reply and we'd duly line up, with a few of the day trippers swelling our ranks.

This particular time they were a motley looking bunch and I was given the job of marking this wee red-haired fellow on the wing who was always latching on to long passes from the big midfielder, whom everybody seemed to listen to.

There's no doubt about it, they had a few good players but we got stuck in under the shadow of the power station.

I seem to remember they took the lead and this red-haired winger was giving me all sorts of problems but, whether it was because of the Export or my boots with only two studs, he seemed to fall about laughing a lot and, come the second half when we swapped ends and some players, we got on top and, by tea time, after 20 minutes one way and 130 minutes the other, I'm sure we were in front 23-17.

By this time the women had lined up and were giving our opposition some stick so it was decided to call full-time and they headed off to board the bus.

Their wee goalkeeper, agile but without teeth, as he joined the rest of his mates, apparently said to one of my pals that they thought we should have been playing in Lishbon.

"What's Lishbon?" my pal asked on the way up the road.

"Do you no ken what Lishbon is?" said one of the others. "That's that new continental formation wi' a scaffy."

"Ye mean a sweeper, ye puddock," said someone else.

"Aye, but whit he was sayin' was that we should've been playin' it," came the exasperated reply.

"Who were they anyway?" another asked. "They had some decent players."

"I asked the wee goalie," said Tom, "and they were a works team, I think, fae Glasgow, but I cannae mind their name. Oh aye, they said they was fae Sheltick."

Oddities
and brevities

The dangers of furry fashion

Fashion has always had the ability to raise a few eyebrows in perplexity. In 1896 though it seems our canine companions were the ones having the greatest difficulty coming to terms with a new fad – the animal skin stole.

One Fife newspaper reported: "A new danger to ladies appears to have arisen through their strange practice of wearing weasels, squirrels, opossums and other animals round their necks as comforters.

"A Burntisland lady who was attacked by a large dog, which suddenly sprang at her face and neck, has recovered damage, but the sheriff threw out the very reasonable hint that the dog thought the boa was a living animal and wished to attack it.

"Possibly enough the dog should have got credit for gallantry in trying to save a lady from some kind of attack. In that case the dog was only one more victim puzzled by the vagaries of feminine fashion."

Uniform approach to a day in court

The local courtroom, particularly the lower levels of summary procedure like the old district set-up, dealt with the less serious offences, but often the more bizarre.

Take for instance the 1904 case of a homeless labourer who found himself charged with breach of the peace. After being locked up in the cell at the Dunfermline burgh police station, the apparently aggrieved man stripped off, piled his clothes next to the cell door, then, using the gas light in the cell, set fire to them.

The Dundee Evening Post reported that when he appeared before the bench the next morning he was partially clad in a policeman's uniform. He received a composite fine of 10s that covered the breach of the peace and burning the cell door.

'Ghost' appears before sheriff

The stranger the tale the further it travels and a bizarre court case from the summer of 1936 found an extensive readership ... as ghost stories tend to do.

This ghoul's 'haunting' was blamed for so terrifying his victim that he brought on pneumonia, and he duly ended up being summoned to Dunfermline Sheriff Court. The offending spectre had actually been revealed as a teenager enveloped in a white sheet.

The youth had been so peeved at his victim's habit of chapping on doors as he made his way home from work that he resolved to teach him a lesson.

Lying in wait, beneath his sheet, the teenager suddenly manifested himself, so scaring his victim that he took to his heels and ran for his life.

"The man ran about half mile to his home, arriving in a state of fright and perspiring freely. Since then he had a bad attack of pneumonia," reported the Sunderland Daily Echo & Shipping Gazette in August 1936. The 'ghost' was fined 10s.

Dad turned in son for a birching

When it comes to 'firsts' there is one Kirkcaldy title that seems to have slipped from memory. It belongs to James More, of Mid-Street, Pathhead.

A teenage printing apprentice, or 'tier-boy', his claim to fame is that, in 1885, he was the first in the Lang Toun to receive the birch.

The power to impose this punishment had been granted some time before but it was reckoned the threat, rather than the act, was a suitable enough deterrent. James' dad disagreed.

The lad had stolen his father's watch, pawned it for 6s, then spent the money. "The father, who appeared in court, said the boy had got altogether beyond his control, and would be obliged if the bailie would give him a flogging," said the Fifeshire Advertiser in October 1885.

The bailie agreed that something had to be done with James and sentenced him to receive five strokes of the birch rod. "The punishment was shortly afterwards administered, and will, no doubt, serve as a warning to others," added the Advertiser.

A case of mistaken identity

In 1905 the law was strict in ensuring children received an education, and failing to send a youngster to school would see you up on charges.

And so it was in March of that year when one father was summoned to Lochgelly Court accused of taking his daughter out of class.

His defence was that the leaving age was 12, and the girl was 14, so there was no case to answer.

The school records indicated the child was 12 so how could he explain the discrepancy in ages between school and home?

That was easy. According to the father, he had 12 children and four of them had been given exactly the same name, hence the confusion ...

Tenants forced to evict children

Life at the turn of the 20th century could be very tough for ordinary folk; for miners it was hard and dangerous, and, by today's standards, it could also be very unjust.

In January 1909, a pit worker from Drumsnick Row, Kelty, appeared before Dunfermline Sheriff Court on charges of contravening the Public Health Act.

The man's offence was permitting overcrowding in his two-roomed house. In all, 12 people lived there, the miner, his wife and their 10 children.

The house had been assigned to him by the Fife Coal Company and an argument was made that it should have been his bosses and not he who was in the dock.

However, obviously fearful for his job, the miner refused to blame his employer.

The sheriff, while stating that it should have been possible for a larger house to be made available and conceding it would be best for a family to stay together, gave the man three weeks to evict some of his older children to solve the overcrowding.

'Little earthquake' rattled Dunfermline

Dunfermline has had its fair share of gas explosions through the years but one of the earliest reported, compared to a "little earthquake", occurred during the summer of 1846 and made the news columns across the United Kingdom.

According to the Bradford Observer a main pipe leaked, allowing a large volume of gas to escape into a sewer under a row of houses where, surfacing, it was ignited by a candle and exploded. The roofs of three properties were blown off, windows smashed, doors torn off the hinges, floors broken, and beds, complete with their occupants, were lifted off the floor. The stones in the street were also forced up.

Miraculously there were no fatalities but one woman had both her legs broken and two other residents suffered minor injuries.

The lad who dug his own grave

There are occasions when truth is certainly stranger than fiction, and even more horrific. One such tale appeared in the Westmorland Gazette in 1858, relating a particularly disturbing Fife story that occurred on a stretch of links.

A group of lads had a rather bizarre and extreme game – burying each other.

There were, according to the Fife Journal where the story first appeared, two aims; the first was to hear who could scream the loudest, the other, to see who could remain underground the longest.

A lad, simply named as 'Brown', helped dig his own 'grave' and, once interred, his pals moved away to the edge of the range of his muffled howls.

A woman returning home spotted the mound with a leg protruding and immediately extricated the youngster.

"To her horror and grief she saw it was her own boy," reported the Gazette, "and, to add to her sorrow, her son was quite dead. His own spade was lying near, and his mouth had been covered with a handkerchief to prevent it being covered with sand and dirt."

Things that go bump in the night, every night

A local newspaper has to always bear in mind it has a family audience. There are certain subjects that need to be covered ... carefully, and there are questions that need to be asked ... delicately.

The Leven Mail shied away from both of these responsibilities in 1957, either believing the former was obvious and the latter self-explanatory, or worried about what response both might produce.

Whatever, the readers were left to ponder just what was going on in an upstairs bedroom in Letham Terrace.

The Town Council had before it a complaint from the downstairs neighbours that they'd had to make up a bed in the living room because of the night-time gymnastics going on above them.

Even the relocation had resulted in the family only managing two nights' sleep in three months – and that was when the upstairs tenants were away.

Apparently the commotion started in the early hours of every morning and continued until it reached a crescendo around 4.30am. There was then a brief respite before a vacuum cleaner was dropped on the floor. This was not switched on until after the 7am news which was played at a volume the downstairs neighbours could hear. Then the vacuuming began.

"Without a reasonable amount of sleep it is impossible to be fit for a day's work," stated the bleary-eyed tenant in a letter. "We would be obliged if you could look into the matter."

The council agreed to write to the upstairs tenants but to also send the housing factor along for a chat given the previous downstairs tenants had fled the property because of the same bedroom manoeuvres reverberating through the ceiling.

Waxing lyrical over bowls

Come September the nights start to draw in and that could present a few problems for sporting occasions in the past.

In 1935 bowlers in Rosyth were involved in a tight tussle at a members' night rinks tournament when darkness fell.

Determined to get the games finished, candles were lit on the green to help the players while the skips fluttered their handkerchiefs over the jacks as markers.

Horrific find on the grazing pasture

Another tale that broke the normal geographic boundaries comes from over a century ago and proves, just as today, anything concerning animals will find an audience.

In June 1895, Fife was enjoying a hot spell but, in Leuchars, the weather was that bit too hot for cattle grazing in a field.

The herd decided to escape the sun and seek the shadows in a low-build shed. With some difficulty 14 beasts managed to squeeze into the shade but the door closed behind them.

"They must have remained packed in this manner for some hours, for when the servant went to feed them he found that 12 were dead and two in a very serious condition," reported the

Stonehaven Journal. "The latter rallied however after being in fresh air for a time. The cattle were very valuable, and the loss will be heavy."

Combat conundrum in the kailyard

The long arm of the law can move in many mysterious ways and in the mid-19th century the decision to pursue one particular prosecution remains perplexing.

The Pittenweem Register in February 1847 reported a case that came before the Justice of the Peace Court in Anstruther. Before the bench was a group of Arncroach wrestlers "summoned to appear to give an explanation as to certain antic manoeuvres which some passer-by had observed in Mr Lundie's cabbage garden".

This passer-by was a stranger to the area and when approaching the Free Kirk, he saw the men tripping, gripping and throwing each other.

Convinced they were trying to murder one another, he ran off and alerted the authorities.

The court heard that the men were all wrestlers who had taken part in the Arncroach games and were enjoying a bit of practice in preparation for the forthcoming Colinsburgh event.

"On this being stated to the presiding judge, there was no more of it."

However, today that report raises a few more questions. Given the incident had occurred a few weeks previously was it normal to have outdoor wrestling practice on a cold day in January? How many wrestlers did Arncroach boast? Didn't anyone ask for an explanation before it was brought to court? How many submissions were made before the knock-out verdict?

Adieu my book! With half reluctant hand
I send thee forth into a bustling scene.
To live thy little week, and be forgot,
As thousands, worthier far,
before have been.

Thomas C. Latto

ABOUT THE AUTHOR

Jerzy (Jurek) Morkis is a Fifer born and raised. Educated at Buckhaven High School and the University of Stirling, he joined the staff of the East Fife Mail in Leven in 1978. He was employed by Strachan & Livingston and then Johnston Press, going on to serve as editor of the Mail and, from 1993, the Fife Free Press. In 2000, he joined a public relations company where he specialised in corporate publications for a number of national companies and organisations. He returned to local newspapers in 2007, again taking the editor's chair of the East Fife Mail before spells at the Fife Herald in Cupar and St Andrews Citizen. He went on to head the community content team for the Johnston Press Scottish portfolio, leaving to follow freelance pursuits in 2017.

Printed in Great Britain
by Amazon

36747901R00059